Social Science
And National Policy

transaction/**Society** Book Series

TA/S-1   *Campus Power Struggle* / Howard S. Becker
TA/S-2   *Cuban Communism* / Irving Louis Horowitz
TA/S-3   *The Changing South* / Raymond W. Mack
TA/S-4   *Where Medicine Fails* / Anselm L. Strauss
TA/S-5   *The Sexual Scene* / John H. Gagnon and William Simon
TA/S-6   *Black Experience: Soul* / Lee Rainwater
TA/S-7   *Black Experience: The Transformation of Activism*
          / August Meier
TA/S-8   *Law and Order: Modern Criminals* / James F. Short, Jr.
TA/S-9   *Law and Order: The Scales of Justice* / Abraham S.
          Blumberg
TA/S-10   *Social Science and National Policy* / Fred R. Harris
TA/S-11   *Peace and the War Industry* / Kenneth E. Boulding
TA/S-12   *America and the Asian Revolutions* / Robert Jay Lifton
TA/S-13   *Law and Order: Police Encounters* / Michael Lipsky
TA/S-14   *American Bureaucracy* / Warren G. Bennis
TA/S-15   *The Values of Social Science* / Norman K. Denzin
TA/S-16   *Ghetto Revolts* / Peter H. Rossi
TA/S-17   *The Future Society* / Donald N. Michael
TA/S-18   *Awakening Minorities: American Indians, Mexican
          Americans, Puerto Ricans* / John R. Howard
TA/S-19   *The American Military* / Martin Oppenheimer
TA/S-20   *Total Institutions* / Samuel E. Wallace
TA/S-21   *The Anti-American Generation* / Edgar Z. Friedenberg
TA/S-22   *Religion in Radical Transition* / Jeffrey K. Hadden
TA/S-23   *Culture and Civility in San Francisco* / Howard S.
          Becker
TA/S-24   *Poor Americans: How the White Poor Live* / Marc
          Pilisuk and Phyllis Pilisuk
TA/S-25   *Games, Sport and Power* / Gregory P. Stone
TA/S-26   *Beyond Conflict and Containment: Critical Studies of
          Military and Foreign Policy* / Milton J. Rosenberg
TA/S-27   *Muckraking Sociology: Research as Social Criticism*
          / Gary T. Marx
TA/S-28   *Children and Their Caretakers* / Norman K. Denzin
TA/S-29   *How We Lost the War on Poverty* / Marc Pilisuk and
          Phyllis Pilisuk
TA/S-30   *Human Intelligence* / J. McVicker Hunt

Social Science And National Policy

Second Edition

Edited by
FRED R. HARRIS

Transaction Books
New Brunswick, New Jersey
Distributed by E.P. Dutton & Co., Inc.

Unless otherwise indicated, the essays in this book originally appeared in *trans*action/Society magazine.

Copyright © 1973
Transaction, Inc.
First edition published 1970.

Transaction Books
Rutgers University
New Brunswick, New Jersey 08903

Library of Congress Catalog Card Number: 72-87663
ISBN: 0-87855-051-8 (cloth); 0-87855-544-7 (paper)

Printed in the United States of America

Contents

Preface   vii

Introduction: 1
Building a New Social Strategy
Fred R. Harris

I. THE PROBLEMS OF POVERTY

Sick Cities—And the Search for a Cure   19
Kenneth B. Clark
Lee Rainwater
Milton Kotler
Herbert J. Gans
Daniel P. Moynihan

Invisible Migrant Workers   43
Dorothy Nelkin

Life in Appalachia—The Case of Hugh McCaslin 59
Robert Coles

In the Valley of the Shadows: Kentucky   83
Bruce Jackson

II. PROGRAMS AND STRATEGIES

On the Case in Resurrection City   113
Charlayne A. Hunter
Reform Proposals   137

FAP Flop: The Fate of Nixon's Welfare
Theodore R. Marmor and *Martin Rein*

Riot Commission Politics   151
Michael Lipsky and *David J. Olsen*

Poverty Programs and Policy Priorities   185
Martin Rein and *S. M. Miller*

III. MECHANISMS

Report on the Social State of the Union   207
Walter F. Mondale

The Case for a National Social Science
Foundation   219
W. Willard Wirtz
Dankwart A. Rustow
Fred Harvey Harrington
John M. Plank
Irving Louis Horowitz and *Herbert Blumer*
Leland J. Haworth
Launor F. Carter

The Need for a National Social Science
Foundation   253
Fred R. Harris

Notes on Contributors   264

Preface

For the past decade, *trans*action, and now **Society**, has dedicated itself to the task of reporting the strains and conflicts within the American system. But the magazine has done more than this. It has pioneered in social programs for changing the social order, offered the kind of analysis that has permanently restructured the terms of the "dialogue" between peoples and publics, and offered the sort of prognosis that makes for real alterations in economic and political policies directly affecting our lives.

The work done in the magazine has crossed disciplinary boundaries. This represents much more than simple cross-disciplinary "team efforts." It embodies rather a recognition that the social world cannot be easily carved into neat academic disciplines; that, indeed, the study of the experience of blacks in American ghettos, or the manifold uses and abuses of agencies of law enforcement, or the sorts of overseas policies that lead to the celebration of some dictatorships and the condemnation of others, can best be examined from many viewpoints and from the vantage points of many disciplines.

The editors of **Society** magazine are now making available in permanent form the most important work done in the magazine, supplemented in some cases by additional materials edited to reflect the tone and style developed over the years by *trans*action. Like the magazine, this series of books demonstrates the superiority of starting with real world problems and searching out practical solutions, over the zealous guardianship of professional boundaries. Indeed, it is precisely this approach that has elicited enthusiastic support from leading American social scientists, many of whom are represented among the editors of these volumes.

The subject matter of these books concerns social changes and social policies that have aroused the long-standing needs and present-day anxieties of us all. These changes are in organizational lifestyles, concepts of human ability and intelligence, changing patterns of norms and morals, the relationship of social conditions to physical and biological environments, and in the status of social science with respect to national policy making. The editors feel that many of these articles have withstood the test of time, and match in durable interest the best of available social science literature. This collection of essays, then, attempts to address itself to immediate issues without violating the basic insights derived from the classical literature in the various fields of social science.

As the political crises of the sixties have given way to the economic crunch of the seventies, the social scientists involved as editors and authors of this series have gone beyond observation of critical areas, and have entered into the vital and difficult tasks of explanation and interpretation. They have defined issues in a way that makes solutions possible. They have provided answers as well as asked the right questions. These books, based as they are upon the best materials from *tran*saction/**Society** magazine, are dedicated to highlighting social problems alone, and beyond that, to establishing guidelines for social solutions based on the social sciences.

The remarkable success of the book series to date is indicative of the need for such "fastbacks" in college course work and, no less, in the everyday needs of busy people who have not surrendered the need to know, nor the lively sense required to satisfy such knowledge needs. It is also plain that what superficially appeared as a random selection of articles on the basis of subject alone, in fact, represented a careful concern for materials that are addressed to issues at the shank and marrow of society. It is the distillation of the best of these, systematically arranged, that appears in these volumes.

THE EDITORS
*tran*saction/Society

Building a New Social Strategy

FRED R. HARRIS

Beginning with Woodrow Wilson, the professor in politics has been a unique participant in the American political scene—the "action intellectual" according to the evocative term coined by Carl Kaysen. For years political parties enlisted the help of such experts and believed that electoral victory might come easier if the people agreed that one party commanded a larger body of more talented experts than the other. But such firm faith in experts even by the experts themselves is now in decline. The passage to a new national mood has been swift.

Two years ago, in the flush of enthusiasm over Apollo landings on the moon, I joined others in calling for an Apollo project in the social sciences. The whole nation saw in the spectacular technological progress of America's space program proof that with the same commitment to meticulous organization, with the same massive funding, we could proceed to eradicate the social problems that plague our

1

planet. Some saw a modern and more effective New Deal in prospect as experts, including social scientists, would again organize to save the country. It was recalled that in 1938 the social sciences received 24 percent of total government expenditures for research, but that by 1950 this had diminished to about 8 percent, and in recent years had fallen to 5 percent or less. All this was supposed to change in a new age for the social sciences.

But instead of a new age there came the sharp shift in popular faith in government by experts. There are, I believe, two solid reasons for this.

First, the continued impact on our national consciousness of the Vietnam experience. Experts brought into government by the Kennedy, Johnson and Nixon administrations conceived and directed our commitment to that miserable war. At first the people believed in their recommendations. But then the gap between the policy they advocated and reality opened too wide. Finally, it became impossible to bear.

Second, the mess in the economy. Economists told President Nixon that the nation could bring inflation under control if only it agreed to a little more unemployment. Then they called for a little more, and still more. Here again, the people at first accepted the recommendations. But then it became clear, even to other economists, that the government's experts did not know what they were talking about. In a flurry of confusion, "Phase II" and price and wage controls followed.

George Wallace is not the favorite politician of people likely to read this book, nor is he mine. But he has a canny ability to sense shifts in the popular mood. When George Wallace speaks out, not only about bussing but also about tax reform or the danger of wire tapping, it is a good sign that people care about these issues.

Today George Wallace is returning to an old theme.

He is again denouncing the "pointy-headed intellectuals" in Washington who try to run the affairs of the common people. He decries supposed thousands of Ph.Ds in the nation's capital walking around "without knowing where they are going." And he contends that these learned men are so lacking in common sense they don't know how to park a bicycle straight.

The audiences love it. Even those who earlier might have rejected these denunciations are tempted to join in because the Vietnam War and the state of our economy have convinced them that the experts no longer know more than the people—if they ever did.

Particularly distrusted are the foreign policy experts from academia. The proponents of ill-conceived "limited war," these men from secure offices in Washington asked the ordinary citizen to send sons, brothers and husbands into an unwinnable war. Meanwhile, for much of this period many of their own sons were draft-exempt because of graduate studies.

The popular realization that the sacrifices for this war were so unevenly spread helped, I believe, to give rise to a curious political phenomenon. Many people became both hawks and doves. They grew more sympathetic to the anti-war movement. And at the same time they urged more support for the military. If the government were going to send their loved ones to Vietnam, then they either wanted total war with practically no holds barred or they wanted the war ended. Public opinion surveyors were surprised to find that many of those who supported Eugene McCarthy in 1968 were also hawks. But in fact our people were being consistent. They wanted the danger ended for our soldiers in Vietnam one way or another—either through an irresistible push for total victory or through withdrawal from Vietnam.

All of which brings us to the theme of this book: the

role of social scientists in understanding and mastering our nation's pressing social and economic problems. Given the popular disaffection with "experts," is now the time to call for an enlarged role at the national level for the social sciences? What "strategy for the social sciences" is suitable to the changed national mood?

Though recent experience may cause us to question the answers experts give us, we all agree the need is for better answers, rather than none at all. An evolving national consciousness of totally indefensible disparities in income and power in America will not permit us to retreat into a know-nothing posture. Popular awareness of economic injustice—unfair taxes and unfair privileges—will compel us to continue, indeed to accelerate the search for solutions. And this means an enhanced role for experts.

But if the time for a national strategy is clear, the core of that strategy is less apparent. We all sense the urgency for movement but we are not quite sure of the direction. I would, therefore, like to suggest a few guidelines which I believe should lie at the core of a national strategy for the social sciences. They include: 1) greater visibility for social problems, 2) conscious posing of alternatives for solving them, 3) institutional support for freer thought and 4) the identification of a new target audience.

Visibility

Charles Dickens in the last century first explained the central importance for the status quo of physically isolating the rich from the poor. In *Hard Times* Dickens noted that the local factory owner did not understand the poverty and social turmoil which lay at the base of England's industrial advance because he never witnessed them. According to Dickens, the owner patterned his life habits, his friendships and even his daily walks so that he only saw around him what would confirm his own views. He avoided the grimy underside of British society because knowledge of it would have compelled him to reject certain features of a society which uniquely favored him and those like him.

A few years ago, Daniel Moynihan wrote "The physical isolation of Negro housing is so near to complete in the United States that it is possible to live in the same city with a million Negro Americans and have only the faintest awareness that they live in distinct neighborhoods and communities that have vastly greater urban problems than those faced by the community at large." Moynihan's observation, so accurate it demands agreement, is nothing more than a modern version of Dickens' earlier insight.

One task of the social sciences, therefore, must be to lay bare the facts and to end the intellectual isolation that prevents us from coping with our problems.

The Need for Alternatives

A growing number of Americans believe they have no control over their future. They feel our system confronts them with ultimatums or confuses them with insignificant details.

Thus, the government may ask electors whether they want a road through a certain section of town. But it never presents them with a number of master plans for solving a community's transportation needs, spells out the economic and social consequences of each and asks local communities to choose. Yet unless this happens, I suggest, people will believe they are being asked trivial questions.

If people are to have any real control over their lives— and they are demanding this—I believe they as well as experts and policymakers must be permitted to think more about the fundamental issues. A national strategy for the social sciences, therefore, must explore an idea of Alvin Toffler that those with expertise be encouraged to draw up for local communities alternative visions of the future. Local organs of government with active citizen participation would then select the kind of community they wished to develop. This would no longer be left to blind chance or outside forces as now is the case.

I realize many liberals fear community control because they worry that communities may decide to do the "wrong thing." Perhaps, liberals argue, local communities will decide to persecute minorities. Given our past, such fears are only too realistic, but look at current Congressional panic over bussing. Can we any longer be so certain that decisions on such sensitive issues made at the national level will be any better? At whatever level of government such decisions are made, I believe the only real protection for our citizens is the Constitution and the willingness of the courts to uphold its provisions. This is why President Nixon's efforts to undermine the Supreme Court's progressiveness are so alarming. With community control, we need a strengthened court system.

Finally, to allay further fears of those who distrust democracy at the local level, I would point out that no one is proposing that the Congress shut its doors and turn all important decisions over to local communities. The problem is more complicated than that.

We can take the racial issue as an example. Our national goal has been and should be a society in which segregation is not tolerated. Today local communities are pressed to accept bussing, which I personally support, as a temporary means of achieving desegregation. The communities in turn see this pressure as an ultimatum and feel that they are being pushed into a corner. Real interests are involved in this issue, so no one pretends that we can solve this problem without controversy. But I believe that passions might cool somewhat if the federal government were to present local communities with alternative routes for arriving at a desegregated school system. The national goal would remain firm but perhaps it would be better, for example, to tell a community that it could achieve this goal either by altering its housing patterns or by bussing. The choice would remain local. There has been some evidence that, when faced with bussing, some communities have become more willing to reconsider their earlier opposition to desegregated housing. Certainly if in achieving a national goal we can leave the selection of means to a local community, we ought to.

More Free Thought

A national strategy for the social sciences would call for more free thought than we have now. Through institutional arrangements it would insure that more than one point of view is heard. And lest some feel that we may depend on the academic world to protect other points of view—that there is no need for the government to worry about this—we might cite the "Velikovsky Affair."

Dr. Immanual Velikovsky was an astronomer who published a book entitled *Worlds in Collision* (1950). Velikovsky maintained that the planet Venus erupted from the planet Jupiter 6,000 years ago and that the trailing meteorites and gases caused terrible devastations on earth which accounted for the biblical plagues and the parting of the Red Sea.

For such heretical views, Velikovsky was ostracized professionally. Several who defended his right to speak were fired from their positions. Professors in several universities threatened a Macmillan textbook boycott unless the publishing house ceased publication of *Worlds in Collision*. One prominent astronomer at Harvard stated: "If Velikovsky is correct, we're all crazy."

Then in December 1962 the U.S. satellite Mariner II passed Venus. It discovered the planet's surface was extremely hot, as Velikovsky had predicted—more than 800 degrees Centigrade—not minus 25 degrees as current theory held. Other fundamental Velikovsky predictions were subsequently proven. Since then, several articles have appeared suggesting Velikovsky may have been right after all.

I cite this case not to side with Velikovsky or against him but only to suggest that his profession showed far less tolerance for unorthodox views than one might hope. The social sciences, even more than the natural sciences, must avoid intolerance; for the soft sciences have no equivalent of a Mariner II to bring to heel strident critics with opinionated views. A national strategy in the social sciences should therefore aim at letting at least several flowers bloom.

Leon Keyserling, former chairman of the Council of Economic Advisors under Truman, has said that most economists in this country belong to a closed shop. Anyone who holds views differing from those held by the established figures in the field seldom gets a hearing, he maintains. In fact, too much unanimity in all professions is now self-imposed. By its actions the federal government must, therefore, take every precaution not to compound the problem; indeed it must actively work in the other direction.

A New Target Audience

Finally, in any national strategy for the social sciences I believe we must reach a new target audience. For decades experts have attempted to talk exclusively to the policy-makers, assuming that only they could make the decisions. It is time for all of us—policymakers and advisers—to begin talking to the people. I believe that they will be making more and more of the decisions that count.

Eight years in the U.S. Senate, two presidential campaigns, service on the Commission for Civil Disorders—these experiences among others have convinced me that this country requires fundamental change if we are to cope with the problems which trouble our political life. Our ability to seek solutions within the existing institutional framework by further tinkering is steadily being exhausted. Solving the basic problems of urban decay, poverty and racial strife will not come about through the establishment of additional New Deal-type programs which burden our institutional framework without changing it.

A poverty program, for example, will not end poverty; but a significant redistribution of income from the rich to the poor might. Honest men in government will not curb the undue political influence of giant corporate interests; but decentralizing our economy and limiting the size of corporations to a level dictated by economic efficiency could. Further appeals to conscience will not end racial injustice; attacking its economic roots would help.

But to do any of these things requires a new national awareness of the need for change. And it is not just the job of the politician to mold that awareness. Social scientists must help in the task. We all must help the majority of the citizens of this country to probe below surface issues to the more important social or economic reality underneath. If we can do this, soon there can be the kind of political consensus in this country necessary to get meaningful change.

Today, however, the social sciences do not have the

recognition from the federal government they need if they are to help mold that awareness. Lack of recognition implies lack of visibility, status and prestige, which in turn tends to lessen the credibility of the social sciences. Neither the intensity and urgency of problems identified by social science research nor the solutions shaped and designed by social scientists will be appreciated so long as governmental structures and programs for supporting the social sciences remain inadequate.

A strategy for the social sciences can come about only when the intensity of social problems, the urgency of related solutions and the relevancy of supporting mechanisms are closely linked together. This coupling process can result from sharp public debate that, for example, identifies alternative programs that could be implemented and various institutions that should then be created. By the use of various forums such debate and dialogue can shape and fashion the goals, priorities and policies that are necessary for the development of a national strategy for the social sciences.

The selection of essays which originally appeared in *trans*action (now called *Society*), a journal that exemplifies the type of forum previously referred to, is arranged in three categories: social problems, proposed alternate solutions and mechanisms. The nature of the interrelationships among the three will ultimately determine the effectiveness of a national strategy.

The book, due to obvious page limitations, is not a definitive work, and the selections do not cover the panoply of problems and issues besetting the nation. Yet the essays are representative of a pervasive major theme—the role of the social sciences in the alleviation and elimination of poverty. Poverty is surrounded by a sea of concepts and processes—urbanization, alienation, frustration, violence,

law and order, repression, permissiveness, justice, accul-
turation, rural deterioration, rural-to-urban population shift,
malnutrition, underclass and so forth. The social sciences
can serve to illuminate these social problems and develop
the requisite tools and methods to remove cancerous social
growths and heal economic wounds that plague America's
democratic values and institutions.

In Part I some of the urban and rural facets of poverty
are exposed. In August 1966 the Senate Subcommittee on
Executive Reorganization chaired by Senator Abraham Ribicoff (D.-Conn.) held a series of hearings on the "biggest
domestic crisis ever," the eruptions of our cities that have
reverberated from sea to shining sea. The main thrust of
the hearings was to determine a strategy for easing the
pressures and tensions in urban America and for instilling
the principles of equality, freedom and justice, which, contrary to the American myth, have still not been extended
to great masses of citizens.

Kenneth Clark poignantly recalls that the success of both
the Manhattan project and the Apollo project was due
largely to a firm national commitment and mandate that
enabled the mobilization of manpower, funds and facilities
to accomplish a finite goal in a relatively short period of
time. These projects, once begun, gained momentum as they
approached their objectives and were not continually pushed
and pulled by shifting coalitions of political forces. (Of
course, the national commitment to these programs held
firm in part because they did not in any way threaten the
balance of political forces in the country. Any important
social reform does.)

In a statement entitled "The Services Strategy vs. The
Income Strategy," Lee Rainwater underscores the theme that
solving the poverty problem should precede tackling the
question of urban management, and in the process he

offers a strong argument on one aspect of social priority setting. More and more people, I believe, will come to share Rainwater's view that it is far more efficient for a government to attack poverty by raising incomes rather than by struggling to expand poorly organized government services.

Milton Kotler asserts that if local government is to be truly local, then the smallest unit of community vitality— the neighborhood—should be the basic building block upon which livable metropolitan areas should be constructed. He calls for establishing neighborhoods as tax-exempt corporations.

"There is Still Time . . . But Not Much Time," cautions Herbert J. Gans, who sees segregation and poverty as the pivotal problems that underlie the sickness of our cities. These two are related and the first to be confronted; tangential palliatives can and should come later.

Daniel Moynihan points out that there is a great crisis in the cities but that, as we have already suggested, few people realize it. In effect, they are largely unaware or would rather divert their attention to inspiring events such as the Apollo program. The lack of visibility of social problems, Dickens' insight, is related to the second-class status which the social sciences have been given in government.

Dorothy Nelkin's essay, "Invisible Migrant Workers," documents the extreme isolation of migrant workers from the community in which they work. And she pointedly concludes:

Open acknowledgment of the existence of a social situation that is dissonant with basic social values would call these conditions into question. As long as the migrant remains out of sight, he is also out of mind. Disturbance may be minimized, but the obvious question remains: Can an invisible problem be resolved?

The rural-to-urban population shift which reached major proportions in the fifties and sixties but which has apparently tapered down in the recent past is indicative of the dynamics and interplay of urban and rural poverty in America. Urban problems are inextricably intertwined with rural problems. Rural migrants to the city, unaccustomed to the tempo of urban life, find it difficult and often impossible to develop a life style that enables them to cope with their new environment. But the problem does not stop there, as was so poignantly pointed out in the report, *The People Left Behind,* prepared by the President's Commission on Rural Poverty. While efforts to deal adequately with urban poverty have been stifled by the lack of visibility of these problems in the American scene, rural poverty has just begun to take on the sense of urgency that it deserves, even among social scientists.

In his article, "Life in Appalachia—the Case of Hugh McCaslin," Robert Coles provides a change of pace with a provocative portrayal of a single individual entrapped in the morass of rural poverty. It is reassuring to encounter a study which avoids broad generalities and concentrates on the individual as a human being rather than as a cipher. It is, after all, the fate of every individual which hangs in the balance of the policy debate on the national antipoverty program.

A companion piece by Bruce Jackson, "In the Valley of the Shadows: Kentucky," establishes that the instruments of control used by the rich against the poor range far beyond the reach of the law. He cites the story of how a welfare department took away the children of two welfare families courageous enough to talk with aides of Senator Robert Kennedy about the inadequacy of welfare payment levels. Depriving these people of their children in effect intimidated others who might complain.

Problems will persist until adequate solutions are found,

in the sense that the measures recommended and the programs proposed are brought to the attention of elected officials and other policymakers. Part II of this book is devoted to articles that suggest solutions to certain aspects of the all-encompassing problems of poverty and other conflicts derived therefrom.

Returning to the theme of visibility, Charlayne A. Hunter, in "On the Case in Resurrection City," opens her chapter by saying: "Resurrection City—where the poor had hoped to become visible and effective—is dead." But, she continues, it was ". . . a moment in history that may yet have a telling effect on the future of this country." In other words, even failure can be fruitful if it is visible failure. The poor people's campaign illustrated how unorganized the poverty-stricken are and how difficult it is for such a group to compete with more highly organized lobby groups that can expertly defend their interests. The field is open for some creative social scientist to advise ways for the poor to gain the kind of representation before Congress which the rich now have.

Theodore R. Marmor and Martin Rein describe the Congress' inability to enact welfare reform. If any lesson emerges from their treatment, it is that politics is too important to be left to the politicians. Until we all, public figures and experts, do a better job of explaining the issues of welfare reform to the voters of this country, we can expect to see the kind of irresponsible political distortion of basic questions which Marmor and Rein have uncovered.

Michael Lipsky and David J. Olsen in "Riot Commission Politics" convey the difficulty presidential commissions face in examining important social problems honestly. Powerful institutions and men always will attempt to place clear constraints on what can be said.

Finally, Martin Rein and S. M. Miller stress the need

for a strategy to eliminate poverty in their chapter, "Poverty Programs and Policy Priorities."

Part III, the last section of the book, is devoted to mechanisms in the form of legislative proposals that have been designed to encourage the development of a strategy for the social sciences. The main argument is that problem identification and solution will not come rapidly and incisively unless federal, state and local institutions exist to provide the social sciences with the level and continuity of support together with the status and prestige that they deserve.

Senator Walter F. Mondale (D.-Minn.) argues in his "Report on the Social State of the Union" for the development of a stronger alliance between social scientists and policymakers. He has introduced legislation that would create a Council of Social Advisors which would prepare a Social Report for the President's transmission to Congress. The act would also create a Joint Congressional Committee on the Social Report. The bill was the subject of extensive hearings in 1967 when introduced as the Full Opportunity and Social Accounting Act and again, in 1969 and 1971, when reintroduced in the 91st and 92nd Congresses as the Full Opportunity Act.

In October 1966 I first introduced the National Foundation for the Social Sciences Act (NSSF). Hearings that year and the subsequent year served to strengthen the case for enactment of the bill. In 1969 I reintroduced the bill, which is cosponsored by 32 senators. The proposed NSSF would, as would the Full Opportunity Act, enhance the status of social scientists by virtue of a legislative mandate. The social sciences would receive a quantum leap in funding and acquire the support of Congress to conduct innovative and sometimes controversial research. It is the latter issue of congressional support that has greatly hampered the growth of the social science program in the National Science Foundation. The foundation had and still has, in spite of a recent reorganization act, a vague mandate for support of these important disciplines.

"The Case for—and Against—A National Social Science Foundation" contains an introductory sketch of the major elements of the bill and the primary issues that have been raised. There follows a series of excerpts from the statements of government officials and noted social scientists who discuss the pros and cons of such an institutional innovation. The section concludes with the statement on the proposal to create a foundation which I made on the floor of the Senate on January 22, 1969.

In summary, the three elements of a national strategy for the social sciences are: 1) highly visible social problems, 2) practical and comprehensive solutions, and 3) governmental mechanisms that serve to identify these problems and encourage the mobilization of funds, manpower and facilities for their solution. In addition, I believe a viable national strategy would follow the guidelines already discussed. In particular, it would respect our democratic creed by always keeping in mind that reforms come from agreement by three groups: policymakers, experts and the people; and of these the people must play the central role.

Poverty today is usually associated with urbanization and the resultant process of dehumanization. Poverty is the concrete jungle of the ghetto with a blade of grass here and there poking through a crack in a sidewalk. Poverty is also rural deterioration and decay and resultant dehumanization. It is rural sidewalks overgrown with weeds and grass.

The rural-to-urban population shift is, to borrow from the words of Karl Marx, a locomotive of history. However, this continuing influx of people to the cities is the result of man-made policies and is not guided by an invisible hand as many laissez-faire demographers would contend. The shift from farm and small town to city is no more inevitable than is poverty. They are both open to solutions.

What types of solutions can and should social scientists provide? First, a better understanding of human and social behavior is imperative, notwithstanding the challenges to conventional wisdom that are likely to result. Basic research should not be neglected, but should receive high priority. The root causes of social problems should be sought out, brought to the surface, and considered by policymakers when designing new programs. These points have been made by the National Commission on Civil Disorders and the National Commission on the Causes and Prevention of Violence. Social scientists should help to design as well as evaluate programs and to sell them to the people. Overall, there is a continuum from knowedge to power with active roles for social scientists to play along this entire spectrum. But if we are to get the political consensus necessary for real change, the people also must gain that knowledge and exercise some power.

Finally, there are new mechanisms needed, especially at the federal level, that will enhance the chances of the social sciences to realize their potential and in the process relieve much of the pressure and strain on the American public. In addition, these sorely needed institutions would encourage debate not only about the needs and uses of the social sciences but about the politics of the social sciences as well. Both components are prerequisites to devising a national strategy for these disciplines.

For such a debate the Full Opportunity Act provides forums—a Council of Social Advisors in the executive branch and a Joint Committee in the legislative branch, and a vehicle—the Social Report. Similarly, the NSSF would report yearly to the Congress on the status and health of the social sciences. These acts would serve to engender viable, stimulating and continuous debate. Without public debate the social sciences cannot attain and retain significant visibility. And, without proper mechanisms, debate cannot occur. In this sense, the form of the dialogue is as important as the content.

This healthy exchange of ideas should help to increase the financial support for and the national visibility of the social sciences to a point where the eradication of some of the great social ills of our time can be accelerated. In this light a concerted effort to develop a national strategy for the social sciences deserves a very high place on our list of national priorities. It is imperative that intellectuals, policymakers and ordinary citizens undertake this effort harmoniously.

United States Senate
Washington, D.C.

Sick Cities...
And the Search for a Cure

INTRODUCTION. In August 1966, after three consecutive summers of urban riots, a Senate subcommittee headed by Abraham Ribicoff (D., Conn.) began inquiring into the role the Federal government should play in easing the problems of the cities—"our biggest domestic crisis ever," as Senator Ribicoff called it. The subcommittee invited about a hundred witnesses, from ghetto residents to big businessmen, to testify. The hearings ended 10 months later, in June, a few weeks before the ghettos of Newark, Detroit, and 70 other American cities erupted.

One major goal of the inquiry, Senator Ribicoff explained, was to help in devising a master plan for dealing with the cities. "Right now," he told *Trans-action,* "we have confusion, a lack of coordination, and programs at cross-purposes. We've passed program after program, all good and necessary programs, but we have no overall objective. We have a piecemeal approach. We need a systematic approach."

In conducting the inquiry, the subcommittee decided to call people in close touch with the problems of the cities, not people who, the Senators thought, saw these problems through a glass, distantly. (This was why the subcommittee saw fit to invite only two economists—though many of the proposals later suggested were economic proposals.) According to Senator Ribicoff, many urban experts had been talking only among themselves, taking in one another's brainwashing. Most of the social scientists invited, therefore, were to speak about what they knew from first-hand experience, from street-corner research. Extracts from the testimony of eight of these social scientists appear on the following pages.

All the social scientists agreed that the problems of the cities stem from racial injustice and poverty—or perhaps from poverty alone. The consensus was that the nation's current urban policies are bankrupt. A number of social scientists called for massive programs to create more jobs for the poor and the unskilled. Several argued for a guaranteed annual income—among them, political scientist Daniel Patrick Moynihan, who suggested family allowances, and sociologist Lee Rainwater, who spoke of his study of life at the Pruitt-Igoe public-housing project in St. Louis and urged that no one's income be permitted to fall below a certain point.

Psychologist Kenneth B. Clark supported the proposal for a guaranteed income, but with deep reservations. He suggested that an agency like the RAND Corporation be created to study urban problems. Sociologist Herbert J. Gans recommended a massive housing program and the creation of many more jobs. Milton Kotler, a political scientist, called for financial aid for neighborhood organizations working on behalf of ghetto residents. Economist Anthony Downs saw little benefit in the proposal for a guaranteed income, and called instead for the dispersal of the ghettos and for more new housing. George Sternlieb, a professor of business administration, endorsed an urban Homestead Act that would permit slum tenants to become property owners.

In short, while the social scientists were almost unanimous in their diagnosis, there was a good deal of disagreement about the best therapy.

Still, the testimony of the social scientists may have accomplished something. Senator Ribicoff went on to introduce a multi-measure "urban America" program, which called for (among other things) new cities to be created and for the government to become the "employer of the last resort." Also included: the establishment of a Congressional agency to evaluate past legislation, a suggestion of Professor Moynihan's. Senator Robert F. Kennedy (D., N.Y.), a subcommittee member, introduced bills to create jobs for slum residents and to construct new housing.

Senator Jacob K. Javits (R., N.Y.), another subcommittee member, even expressed limited support for a guaranteed income—a proposal endorsed by many of the social scientists. In an interview, Senator Javits said: "We may have to modify it, but the income maintenance proposal needs to be looked into urgently." Senator Ribicoff had shown interest in the idea early in the hearings, but apparently was swayed by the criticism he heard: "As Dr. Clark told us, the poor man needs to feel his individual worth. He needs wages, not handouts."

Perhaps the basic value of the hearings, though, lay in the very fact that they were held. They symbolized a mounting commitment on the part of certain not uninfluential Senators to solve the cities' problems. Looking back over the inquiry, for example, Senator Ribicoff maintained that action "is more urgent than ever. Nothing has changed.

It's only worse—this summer has proved that. But with this war in Asia, Congress is avoiding new programs costing money. Eventually Congress will have to face up to the explosive problems we exposed—and act to resolve them." Eventually? "Eventually," Senator Ribicoff emphasized, "is *today.*"

THE URBAN NEGRO IS THE 'URBAN PROBLEM'

Daniel P. Moynihan

The central thesis of these hearings is that American society is facing an urban crisis. I seriously doubt that even a significant minority of the American people believe any such thing. The foundations of disbelief are varied but convergent. The principal one is that for a solid quarter century the great mass of Americans have experienced a steadily rising standard of living, in a measure without parallel in history. This rising level of well being has been accompanied by and in large measure has consisted of improvements in housing, transportation, education, health, recreation, and other "urban" amenities which are now said to be in a state of crisis, but which most persons know to be in a vastly better condition now than in times past. I believe it fair to say that this popular impression corresponds to whatever reality is reflected in our standard national statistics, and that a great many students of cities, however urgent they may feel is the need for further improvement, will nonetheless agree that things are far better now than they have ever been.

What then is the case for "crisis"? It rests largely, I believe, on three congeries of facts which are only somewhat related to each other, but which tend to be perceived with equal concern by persons interested in this sort of thing.

■ The first set of "facts" consists of assertions that American cities are ugly, incoherent, sprawling cultural wastelands. Los Angeles is the preferred example, and with good reason.

■ The second set of facts is addressed to the severe financial strains which most central cities are experiencing.

■ The third set concerns the growth of a large Negro lower class in those cities, a group that many seem to feel is less assimilable than lower class immigrant groups that have preceded it, and which recently has erupted in sporadic mass violence. . . . The appearance of large numbers of lower class Negroes in Northern cities has led many persons to assert that we are in the grip of a unique problem. It seems to me that it is not yet clear whether this is so, but it may turn out that it is. In the meantime I would certainly agree with James Q. Wilson that "for the present, the urban Negro is, in a fundamental sense, *the* 'urban problem.'"

But even here one is impressed with how easy it is for the great number of Americans to remain quite unaware of any such situation. The physical isolation of Negro housing is so near to complete in the United States that it is possible to live in the same city with a million Negro Americans and have only the faintest awareness that they live in distinct neighborhoods and communities that have vastly greater "urban" problems than those faced by the community at large. And such is the hold of race on the American mind that it becomes entirely too easy simply to assume that Negroes will act differently from whites, an assertion one hears increasingly from Negroes as well. I have often wondered, for example, what would be the reaction of the business community if it were reported that the "proletariat" were rioting in Los Angeles, or Cleveland, or Rochester, or wherever, instead of Negroes. Would there not be a deeper tremor of concern? It is a vicious but persisting fact of American life that white Americans accept as almost natural the fact that Negro Americans are mistreated and that in response they misbehave. And somehow whites contrive to dislike Negroes on both grounds.

In any event, it remains the case that only a limited number of Americans see contemporary problems as a result of the malfunctioning of that system of economic and social relationships that are defined as urban.

But there is yet another source of reluctance to accept the reality and urgency of urban problems which is more difficult to isolate—and impossible, I should think, to prove —that I would nonetheless presume to bring to your attention. I would call it the "crisis in confidence" with regard to the efforts that have already been made to deal with the urban problem.

. . . The American public supports a fantastic array of social services, and does so in ever larger amounts. The issue, then, is not whether, but which. Thus, with regard to persons living in or near to poverty, a fundamental issue is to choose between a strategy of services, which Shriver's proposal would entail, as against a strategy of income. The amounts of money a Project Keep Moving would require are in the range of those that would be needed to establish a national family allowance. I can imagine a good argument being made that if there is an extra thousand dollars a year to go round for every family in the nation, or every poor family, that the best thing would be to give them the cash and let them spend it on things they think they need most—which might well be formal education for many, but would surely be more varied than any formula laid down in Washington would permit. In any event, to propose spending the money on services, which such research as we have suggests will produce little or no effect, is to risk being thought ridiculous or worse by members of the public, and we would delude ourselves if we did not see that this judgment has already been reached by large numbers. . . .

I believe our difficulty here has two quite different components. The first is that our commitment to evaluation research is, as Peter Rossi states, fundamentally ambivalent; one of attraction and fear, trust and distrust. This is so not only because research of this kind can blow up in an administrator's face when it turns out his programs show little or none of the effects they are supposed to achieve, but more importantly, because in areas of social policy, facts are simply not neutral, however much we would hope to treat them as such. In social science, data are political. Most social arrangements rest on assumptions about the "facts" of a given situation. To challenge such facts is also to challenge those social arrangements, as Louis Wirth has observed. As distinguished a social scientist as Walter B. Miller has suggested that because this is so there may even be "a direct incompatibility between careful evaluative research and the political process." Certainly we would agree that research findings, which are almost invariably complex, cautious, and qualified, and often indicate the most modest impacts, are hardly attuned to political rhetoric.

The second source of difficulty, however, is of quite a different nature. It is that up until now the executive branch of the federal government, and the executive branch in American government in general, has had a virtual monopoly on the product of evaluation research. Congress, the state legislatures, the city councils, are simply told what have been the results of such research. They do not have to agree, but they are hard put to disagree.

There is nothing sinister about this state of affairs. Serious evaluation research, as I have said, is only just reaching the state of a developed—as against an experimental—technique. Inevitably it has been sponsored in the first instance by executive departments. However, because the findings of such research are not neutral, it would be almost dangerous to permit this imbalance to persist. There are a number of reasons. First, and most important, the Congress and other legislative bodies are put at a considerable disadvantage. A major weapon in the "arsenal of persuasion" is in effect denied them. Second, the executive is exposed to the constant temptation to release only those findings that suit its purposes; there is no one to keep them honest. Third, universities and other private groups which often undertake such research on contract are in some measure subject to constant if subtle pressure to produce "positive" findings. The simple fact is that a new source of knowledge is coming into being; while it is as yet an imperfect technique, it is likely to improve, and if it comes to be accepted as a standard element in public discourse it is likely to raise considerably the level of that discourse. This source of knowledge should not remain an executive monopoly.

How is Congress to respond? I would offer a simple analogy. In the time this nation was founded, the principal form in which knowledge was recorded and preserved was in printed books, and accordingly in 1800 Congress established the Library. Over the next century, techniques of accounting and budgeting developed very rapidly, and in 1921 Congress established the General Accounting Office. I would like to suggest that Congress might now establish an Office of Legislative Evaluation which would have the task of systematically evaluating the results of the social and economic programs enacted by it and paid for out of public monies. Such an office could be established as a separate agency, or it could be located in the Library of Congress or the General Accounting Office. But the essential feature must be that it will be staffed by professional social scientists who will routinely assess the results of government programs in the same manner that the GAO routinely audits them. It should not be expected that their findings will be dramatic or quick in coming, or that they will put an end to argument—just the contrary is likely to occur. But the long-run effect could be immensely useful. The Congress could develop in its terms a series of data comparable to the social indicators which the executive branch is now developing. I would like to make clear also that such an office should concern itself as much with matters such as the farm program or the merchant marine program as with those concerned with poverty or health or education.

THE INTERESTS OF THE PRIVILEGED ARE AT STAKE

Kenneth B. Clark

The first approach to dealing with problems of slums, which became the basis of our social welfare system, is by trying to help these people in "Lady Bountiful" style— charity, community centers, or things of that sort. It is clear that this did not work—with increased social services, we got increased pathology. The predicament of people in the slums did not improve as a result of social services; the only thing that happened was that the social agencies and social services became more affluent.

The antipoverty program is another attempt to deal with the problems of the slums, and it seems to be based on a new approach. Unlike the older social service approach which tried to do things for people or give charity to people, the core of the antipoverty program, when I was involved in trying to develop this rationale, was that people should be helped to help themselves. Community action was considered the key new approach to rehabilitating people in the slums.

I think two or three years of evidence would lead to a candid assessment that this has not worked any better than the old social service approach. The emphasis on community action for effective solution of slum problems seems to be more verbal than actual. Wherever we found any attempt at significant community action as part of the antipoverty programs, almost invariably political considerations intervened to truncate or control or restrict the extent of community action which local political figures would permit. . . .

When our society is serious about solving any given social, economic, or military problem, it mobilizes the best brains and experts in the particular field and provides them with the financial resources, the facilities, and the power necessary to understand and to solve that basic problem. This was certainly the approach which we used in developing the atomic and nuclear bombs, and it was the approach which we used in achieving our successes in exploration of outer space. This was the basis upon which the Air Force set up the RAND Corporation 20 years ago. . . .

I think the budget is about as good an index of the priority society gives various problems as one can find. Our space program and our Vietnam war have budgetary supports which indicate tremendous seriousness. Our antipoverty programs have budgetary indications of secondary, tertiary, peripheral priorities, and I don't think that we will solve the problems of our inner cities by relegating them to peripheral priorities. If we are really serious about solving the problems of our ghettos and reversing the pathology and plight of our cities, we must use the same approach we use in these other areas.

I am proposing—and am now involved in trying to set up—at least the nucleus of a RAND Corporation type of center for the study and solution of urban ghetto problems. This center in its initial form is an independently funded consortium in the fields of social science, municipal and public affairs, consumer interests. Experts will be brought together to monitor all areas of governmental services and programs to assure that the rights of the poor, the victims of our slums and ghettos, and the underprivileged in our cities are not ignored; that these people are no longer short-changed as they have callously been in the past; that their share in the economic and political benefits of the society will not be lost or preempted by others; and that their civil, legal, and constitutional rights are not ignored or disregarded because of their lack of power to protect themselves. It is my hope that these specialists would function on behalf of the poor in ways similar to the ways in which more privileged middle class individuals and groups function for themselves. I am trying to determine whether it is possible to systematize and organize empathy. The primary and exclusive goal of these experts would be the representation and assistance of the poor—not representation in the literal sense of being elected by them, but of being concerned with their welfare as if it were our own that was at stake (and, by the way, I don't think this is an abstract point).

I think that we are going to become serious about the problems of our cities and our slums and our ghettos only when more privileged people understand that the pathology of the ghettos cannot be confined to the ghettos and that the interests of the privileged are at stake. There is no immunity to the consequences of squalor.

THE SERVICES STRATEGY VS. THE INCOME STRATEGY

Lee Rainwater

There seem to me to be two different kinds of urban problems, although each deeply affects the other. Efforts to solve the general problems of *urban management* will forever be frustrated—or at least much, much more costly—without a solution to the *problem of poverty,* both urban and rural. Unless the poverty problem is solved, every urban service will have to be seriously distorted and fragmented in order either to avoid or to take special account of the problems posed by having an "other America." For this reason, as well as for reasons of simple human justice, first priority in dealing with urbanization as our major domestic problem should be given to the elimination of poverty.

The elimination of poverty has a very simple referent. It means that the present income distribution in the nation —in which a small group of the population earns a great deal of money, a large proportion earns a more moderate amount of income, and a small proportion earns very little —must be changed by moving that bottom portion up into the middle category. In short, the current diamond-shaped income distribution must be changed into one which has the shape of a pyramid. I'm speaking here about family income rather than individual income.

There is certainly nothing wrong with a teenage boy earning $1.50 an hour while he goes to school or while he learns a trade. But there is something very wrong about that kind of income for a head of a family with two or three children, or for a man who would like to be the head of a family but cannot afford to be.

This redistribution would channel national income, particularly the yearly increment in national income, to families in the lower 30 to 40 percent of the population, so that a family income floor is established which is not too far below the median income for American families as a whole. If we can accomplish this, we will have succeeded in creating an urban society in which, while problems may still be difficult, they will not seem nearly so insoluble, because we will not have to plan for two kinds of Americans, the average American and the deprived American, as we do now.

It seems to me that there are basically two strategies implicit in the various programs and suggested plans for doing something about poverty: One, by far the most entrenched at present, might be called the *services strategy,* and the other, the *income strategy.*

The services strategy involves the design of special services for the poor. The problem with the services approach is that to a considerable extent it carries the latent assumption that either the poor are permanently poor and, therefore, must have special services, or that the poor can be changed while they are still poor, and that once they have changed, they will then be able to [function] in ways that will do away with their poverty. I think these assumptions are extremely pernicious ones.

One problem with the services approach is that the priority of needs of the poor is categorically established when the service programs are set up and funded. For example, the federal public housing program provides a service to each household in Pruitt-Igoe in the form of a subsidized apartment that costs about $545 a year—that is the subsidy. This subsidy amounts to a fifth of the mean family income of the tenants in the project. It is very likely that from the point of view of the needs of many of the families who live in Pruitt-Igoe that $545 could be put to much better use.

For another example, the Council of the White House Conference "To Fulfill These Rights" recommended that one program to help do away with Negro disadvantage could be to increase the average school expenditure per child $500 per year. Consider a poor family with three or four school children. Such an increase would mean devoting $1,500 to $2,000 a year to better educational facilities for that family's children. Yet, might it not be that, because of its effect on the family environment, an increase of $1,500 to $2,000 in that family's income would have as much or more educational effect on those children than would a comparable expenditure of resources in the school?

Finally, special programs for the poor are extremely difficult to design so that they do not have the effect of furthering the stigmatized status of the poor. To design services which do not stigmatize at the same time that they try to serve seems to pose tremendous political, administrative, and human engineering tasks, for which past experience gives us little reason to believe we have the skills.

Most of those who have studied the actual operation of service programs catering to an exclusively lower class clientele have been impressed by the demeaning and derogation of the poor that goes along with the service. The principal power that the poor want is the power of money in their pockets to make these choices as they see fit and as the needs of their families dictate.

The second poverty elimination strategy, the income strategy, goes a long way toward avoiding the difficulties that past experience suggests are inherent in the services strategy. Here the task is to develop a set of economic programs that have the direct result of providing poor families and individuals with an adequate income. There are good reasons from the social science information now available to us for believing that the most powerful and immediate resource to assist the poor to cope with their problems, not only the problems of economic disadvantage, but all of the dependent problems of community pathology, individual lack of motivation, and the like—the most powerful resource is income.

We know, for example, that when a man has a job and an adequate income, he is more respected in his home, and he is less likely to desert or divorce his wife. If one wishes to reverse those effects of lower class adaptations that are unconstructive, the most direct way of doing it is to strike at the root of the problem—at the lack of an income sufficient to live out a stable "good American life" style.

Having said this, I leave the field of sociological expertise because the problems are then ones that require the technical competence of an economist. Those economists who have pursued this line of thinking in studying the problem of poverty have suggested that an income strategy requires three elements:

■ An aggregational approach—that is, tight full employment—with a low, a very low, real unemployment rate—that is, an unemployment rate that takes into account labor force dropouts.

■ Second, a structural approach, which compensates the tendency for unemployment among low skilled workers to remain at high levels even when over-all unemployment is low. Such an approach would require that federal programs to bring about full employment be tied to guarantees of labor force entry jobs for unskilled men, and guarantees of training on the job to upgrade those skills. In this context, a high minimum wage would also be necessary and would not have the negative effect of hastening the replacement of men by machines.

■ Finally, an income maintenance program, which fills in

the income gap not touched by the tight full employment programs. The income maintenance program would be required for families with a disabled or no male head, and where the wife should not work because of the ages or numbers of the children.

Such a program could take the form of family allowances or a negative income tax or an annual guaranteed income, but in any case should involve a major reorganization of the government's current income maintenance programs, notably ADC and other types of public assistance, since these current programs are by far the most stigmatizing poverty programs now in existence.

If the first two employment strategies were as successful as some economists feel they might be, the dollar investment in an income maintenance program could be quite small. However, such a program would have considerable long-run importance, since it would serve as proof of a more permanent national commitment to a more equal income distribution, and as a yearly goal to the federal government to plan the economy in such a way that no more than a very small number of families are without an adequate bread-winner. . . .

MAKING LOCAL GOVERNMENT TRULY LOCAL

Milton Kotler

. . . The facts of urban poverty are these: Unemployment is rotten, education is poor, health is bad. Together, these factors impose a menacing condition. Yet there is encouragement in this committee's deliberation, and indeed in recent legislative moves. It represents a commitment within the government to apply some of its wealth and know-how to this urban crisis.

Now the choice is between the existing despair and the new hope. How is the task to be done? What is the proper method of action to rebuild the slum? What is the proper role of different agents of change—public and private, federal, state, and local—to assist this measure? I think the crucial question is whether we find the method. The country has wealth, but we are often short on concept. The real test is to find the concept of change and apply our resources to it.

To my mind, that concept is neighborhood self-governing decision. The neighborhood, constituted as a non-profit, tax-exempt, democratically structured corporation with its own assembly, officials, and revenues, is the principal agent of change to rebuild our slums into a legal community of culture, freedom, and prosperity. The neighborhood must become a legal community of self-help and self-governing decisions with sufficient capacity to relate to other organizations, public and private, for the resources and assistance to build a better city.

There is a lot of talk today about the neighborhoods being gone, not very viable in the new technological age. I grant the scepticism, but I also want to introduce the fact that the neighborhood is a living reality in the lives of people who live in our cities. The neighborhood is the last remaining unit, territorial unit, of public confidence in our cities.

There is often little confidence in the city government. The neighborhood is the last unit of public confidence, and therefore, one must apply to that unit of public confidence the instrumentalities of legal self-governing decision and resources to act on this problem.

The neighborhood must be strengthened by organization and legal incorporation. It must be legitimized by democratic structure and public authority over resources to decide and act on specific local matters of the neighborhood. It might be 7,000 people or indeed in our densest, largest cities it is quite conceivable to view neighborhoods as groups of 100,000 or more.

The neighborhood as a legal community must become the principal agent in rebuilding its locality and governing the public matters that intimately affect the lives of its residents. Further, neighborhood corporations must be responsible to each and every resident through democratic structure, and also responsible, through their legal agency and powers, to outside authorities, public and private.

Our cities are too large. Today New York is the size our nation was when it was first constituted. Today many cities are larger than states were in an earlier day. . . .

Today, the field of humanity and popular hope in the slums is the territory of their neighborhood community. The expression of hope is through neighborhood decision. Structure that hope into the neighborhood corporation, and let that hope exercise itself legally and practically upon the material conditions of poverty. If the impoverished conditions of slum life are political, and indeed all the poor conditions constitute a political condition of oppression, the method of change is simply political independence and freedom, which incorporates the neighborhood for decision, and uses the resources of technology and the wealth of a nation to do the task.

■ The neighborhood area must be organized as a tax-exempt corporation based on one man-one vote assembly and membership.

■ It must be territorially bound.

■ It must be democratically structured on the basis of assembly, officials, and funding.

■ It must be formed to govern something public.

The neighborhood corporations must have authority to

govern certain matters of social service or economic development that intimately affect their local life. The neighborhood corporation must relate, in its practice of decision and of management of services, to all appropriate public and private agencies and organizations. It must be a part of the way of performing public services in the city.

This argument is practical as it reflects two years of experience in Columbus [Ohio] in the ECCO project. ECCO (the East Central Citizens Organization) is today a tax-exempt neighborhood corporation of 7,000 residents in a poor area of the city. Its territory is one square mile. Its population is 70 percent Negro and 30 percent white. Unemployment is high. The median income is about $3,000. Housing is substandard. And in many respects it corresponds to poverty areas elsewhere.

Today, however, ECCO is no longer a desperate slum, because of its corporation and the action and decision of its citizens in assembly, council, and administration, in deciding the affairs of that community. ECCO is not just a poor community, but a poor community building its prosperity through dignity and independence. For the first time in the lives of its residents, that neighborhood community is an integral part of the life of the city. . . .

ECCO has the support of its people and the city. There are no riots in ECCO because ECCO has the authority to decide and govern affairs. Politicians do speak to ECCO in assembly and council. There is communication between the people of ECCO and the city, because ECCO is itself a government and has representative elective officials. . . .

This experience, I think, evidences the need for this new unit, the neighborhood corporation. I would suggest that the federal government currently fund the governing structures of neighborhood corporations around the country. . . . Direct funding can be used in many cities to set up the governing structure of neighborhood corporations, which in our case runs about $150,000.

Once formed, the neighborhood corporations can move toward delegate agencies to local community action organizations for program funding. But also under other legislation for housing grants, education grants, and so forth. In that connection I would sincerely urge a legislative thrust at amending such legislation in housing, labor, and other departments to develop the ability for the federal government to grant directly to neighborhood corporations as non-profit agencies. . . .

"THERE IS STILL TIME . . . BUT NOT MUCH TIME"

Herbert J. Gans

On the basis of 15 years of research and practice as a sociologist and city planner, I am convinced that the major problems of the city have almost nothing to do with the city. Instead, they can all be traced, directly and indirectly, to two sources, the *poverty* and the *segregation* faced by an increasing number of city dwellers. Poverty and segregation are the basic causes of slums, for when people cannot afford decent housing and are discriminated against, they *must* overcrowd the oldest and least desirable buildings of the city. The despair that results from poverty and segregation encourages such desperate acts as delinquency, addiction, and family and personal breakdown, as well as ghetto unrest and rioting. These acts help to encourage the white middle class exodus to the suburbs, and this in turn deprives cities of municipal revenues, and downtown retail districts of profitable customers, which hasten their decline. And the fear of poor and nonwhite city voters nurtures the suburban opposition to metropolitan solutions, as well as the backlash voting patterns of blue and white collar urban residents whom I call the not-so-affluent.

The urban crisis is also rural, for the cities attract, as they always have, people who seek relief from worse poverty and segregation in rural areas. The crisis is thus national; it has to do with economic and social inequality in the nation as a whole. That crisis is above all economic, for it is *poverty* that causes social and individual breakdown, and it is the *poverty* and *poverty-induced behavior* of the slum dwellers, not their race, which brings on the fears that drive affluent whites to the suburbs and not-so-affluent ones to violent opposition against open housing. And urban poverty is in turn largely the result of *unemployment* and *perhaps even more of underemployment;* of being limited to underpaid, insecure, dirty, dead-end jobs.

Consequently, the best—and probably the only—solution for America's urban problems is to enable the poor, the unemployed, and the underemployed to obtain the jobs and incomes that will incorporate them into the affluent society. Once this is accomplished, the remaining problems of the city can be solved more easily, and the class-based opposition to racial integration will disapppear. . . .

The experience of urban renewal and public housing suggests that neither program has helped the poor significantly. In too many cities, where inexpensive housing was already in short supply, the clearing and rehabilitation of slums only forced poor people to pay yet higher rents, often in other slums. Incidentally, urban renewal did not even achieve its aim of luring middle class people back to the city. And moving poor people into public housing did not solve their basic problems. It is clear that just giving poor people better housing cannot eliminate their poverty.

We must therefore turn our approach upside down: to eliminate the poverty of the poor so that they can afford decent housing and solve their other problems as well. Consequently, the prime goal of any housing program must be to create jobs for the unemployed and underemployed even while it creates good housing for them and renews the cities.

Such a housing program should consist of three elements. First, it should encourage the building of millions of new federally subsidized "moderate" and "middle" income, racially integrated units in cities, suburbs, and new towns, much like the units already being built with the help of FHA's nonprofit housing program, and other federal and state subsidies. Second, rent supplements should be provided on a much larger scale to enable poor people to choose new or older units, and third, the dwellings and neighborhoods of the slums must be rebuilt and rehabilitated.

This housing program should create as many new jobs as possible. Moreover, it would enable the recipients of these jobs to choose new or old housing like all other Americans, and [even more] to do so with rent supplements. It would also press forward on urban and suburban integration at the same time as the ghettos are rebuilt for those who prefer to remain in familiar neighborhoods. I suspect that if nonwhite people had free choice in housing, many would remain in their present neighborhoods, and only a small number would now choose the suburbs. Consequently, the suburban fear of inundation by former slum-dwellers is groundless. I suspect that this is the case, but because of the lack of housing and other urban research, we do not really know, just as we do not know much about the real effects of urban renewal, or about what people— poor, affluent, and not-so-affluent—want and need in their communities. . . .

New income and job-creating programs will be costly, but A. Philip Randolph's Freedom Budget suggests that the funds can come just from the increases in national productivity in the next decade. They will also be controversial, but if they are not carried out, we can expect a steady rise in the self-destructive and anti-social behavior of the city's poor, as well as in demonstrations and riots, especially if other Americans continue to become more affluent. . . . Increased pathology and violence are not only social dangers *per se,* but they will surely be met by public demands for repressive actions and for retrenchment in governmental anti-poverty efforts, and repression and retrenchment can only result in yet more pathology and violence in return. This would create a vicious circle of pathology, repression, more pathology, more repression, that could spiral into really widespread pathological behavior and open class warfare in the years to come. Then the taste of affluence will be bitter, and the American way of life not worth living even for the affluent. . . .

October 1967

Invisible Migrant Workers

DOROTHY NELKIN

Early last summer, the soft earth of a California peach orchard yielded the bodies of 25 nameless murder victims. Their anonymity was made less astonishing by the discovery that all the dead men were migrant farm workers— a group whose isolation from society is well known. Indeed, the accounts of the lives of migratory workers from *Grapes of Wrath* to *Harvest of Shame* have described these people as invisible to the rest of American society. But are they invisible even to each other? Was there no one to miss the slain men? Surely no group can be so alienated as to accept murder rather than call the police—or can it?

To discover just what social forces could account for the namelessness of migrant faces, a four-year participant-observation study was made of black migrant farm workers in the northeastern United States. The findings suggest that migrant invisibility is systematic—that it is controlled by mechanisms both from within and without the migrant group.

Though the migrant worker may live in a camp five months out of a year, his communication with the permanent community is kept at a minimum. First, he is often physically isolated. Camps are usually located in out-of-the-way sites several miles from the nearest town. And since most migrants were brought North on a bus by a crew leader, they rarely have their own means of transportation. If community facilities near camps are used there are often separate stores and laundromats so that migrants are segregated from local residents. Other more subtle barriers also separate the migrants from local populations. For example, the illegal sale of alcohol in camps is not only ignored, but sometimes encouraged in the hope that the migrants will drink in camp rather than in the town bars.

Sodus Village is the center of one such agricultural area; there are 50 labor camps in the township with facilities for housing about 1,000 workers. Many of their employers live in the village, which has a population of 1,233 of age 14 or over. Even though migrants use the town laundromats and gas stations, shop in the stores and drink at the local bar, a random sampling of the townspeople showed that over two-thirds had no direct contact with the workers. Nearly 10 percent said they had never noticed a labor camp nearby. Even among the majority who were aware of the camps, having noticed them from the highway, knowledge of life within the camps was vague or nonexistent. Despite their physical presence in the community they are not a part of it. The migrant is an outsider, an element to be dealt with as a problem.

An agricultural community may have church or lay groups concerned with migrant welfare. Their interest ranges broadly from prayer and indignation to the management of day schools and child-care centers. Old clothes, money and transportation services are often provided when there are people with the energy and ability to organize collections. It was found, however, that the clergy were more interested in social action programs than were their parishioners. One minister had been working with migrants for several years and, despite a highly conservative parish consisting largely of growers, devoted considerable energy to providing social services in nearby labor camps. His parishioners had not complained about his activities with the migrant workers, but they did not volunteer to participate personally in his programs. Torn between his desire to help the migrants and his obligations to his parish, he hesitated to spend much time on migrant-worker problems. When asked if his parishioners would mind if migrants came to the church, he replied that the question never came up. Since there was absolutely no social contact between the two groups, the migrants would "just not be interested in coming." He strongly asserted that migrants "do better in their own situation," and that he would not consider encouraging a migrant to attend services in his church. His activities consisted primarily of showing films and bringing athletic equipment to the camp. But the migrants were apathetic toward his efforts, and he felt that he had failed to accomplish anything of significance. Totally frustrated, he was waiting for mechanization to solve the problem by drying up the migrant labor stream.

The habit of ignoring controversial or disturbing problems in a community is seldom a conscious one but may surface during a crisis. In one agricultural area, a migrant child-care center was about to close in the middle of the summer because the public-school building in which it was located was no longer available. A local minister was under pressure to find an alternate location. When asked about the possibility of using his Sunday-school building, he said it would be impossible since there was a very small septic tank and the system would be ruined if more people used the toilets. He finally admitted, however, that the vestry was more liberal than the parishioners, who were quite willing to supply old clothes as long as the migrants remained in their camps; caring for their children on church property was another matter.

The success of other agencies concerned with migrant welfare has been similarly limited. State and federally sponsored antipoverty programs have been organized to change the migrant labor situation, but social workers have had difficulty in communicating with their clients and arousing interest in the programs provided. Social workers tend to assume that the value of their offerings is self-evident, that they need only bring what they think is necessary into the camps, and the migrants will welcome them. They are often dismayed to discover this is not the case. There are a number of possible reasons for this breakdown in communications: the attitude of migrants commonly labeled apathy, the irrelevance of the particular program offered and the fear that outsiders are only introducing one more exploitative mechanism.

A more important factor in the failure of most programs, however, is that client invisibility is built into the sponsoring organizations themselves. The experience of one social-work organization will serve as an example. Though its stated purpose was to improve conditions for migrants and to enable them to deal knowledgeably and effectively with society, agency staff members indicated that they were perpetually frustrated by lack of rapport with migrants in the camps they visited. The director of this agency knew little about his clients and seldom visited the camps in which his program operated, working instead through subordinate field instructors. In spite of his limited activity in the field, he ran the program in a centralized and authoritarian manner, and the field instructors, who had day-to-day familiarity with the camps, often found themselves disagreeing with his decisions.

For the most part, field instructors occupied their time playing with children and showing films, many of which were inappropriate to the audience. For example, one oil-company advertisement exalted the American farmer and pictured him as a national hero, fair and blond, driving his tractor across the many acres of his farm. Another was a sex education film originally developed for a middle-class school audience.

Field instructors were constrained by the centralization of decision-making in the organization and by inadequate preparation for work with migrants. Training sessions had been conducted by teachers who had experience in industrial personnel work, but who had no knowledge of problems peculiar to the migrant system. Thus, much energy was deflected to handling problems within the organization itself.

This agency and others are hampered by their dependence on local authorities. They must adjust their activities more to established community interests than to the migrants who make few conspicuous demands. Thus, their primary goals become the avoidance of disruption and the maintenance of a level of satisfaction which will minimize demands. At the same time they must make sure that educational programs, health care and other activities do not interfere with the harvest.

National or statewide church organizations occasionally employ social workers to deal with migrant labor problems. They select personnel who will work quietly, offering services that will keep the migrants happily ensconced in the camps. One social worker regularly tried to call attention to problems in the camp. His organization disapproved, and he was eventually asked to submit his resignation.

Other programs have been hampered by the insensitivity of social workers themselves, some of whom have been observed conducting themselves in camps as if their clients were not there. One such worker talked to a friend while showing movies one evening. He was unaware that their conversation was interfering with the sound track. The viewers, distracted by the voices, kept looking back, but the two men continued to talk in a normal tone until the end of the film. In another case, a social worker invited a researcher to see some migrant rooms. When knocking produced no response from the occupant of one room, he went in anyway. He asked another woman if he could show her room to the observer but had opened the door and was inside before she had a chance to answer. The woman said nothing. It did not occur to him that his actions were an invasion of privacy and later, oblivious to the people nearby, he declared that this was his favorite camp because "people are very friendly and there is never any threat of trouble."

Even genuinely concerned volunteers find themselves constrained by community pressures. One woman had written a letter to the welfare department concerning incidents in which migrants were refused medical attention. When inspectors were sent to investigate the matter, delegations of concerned citizens visited her home to ask her to retract her statements. Other outspoken volunteers have been effectively controlled by their organizations and reassigned to innocuous jobs. One black social worker described by his co-workers as "not very well liked here" was under pressure from colleagues who feared he would "cause trouble." He had been critical of interminable meetings and of other social workers who avoided going to the camps. In the camps, however, where he distributed Social Security cards and dispensed information about jobs and events outside the camp, observers noted that he was more effective and had closer rapport with the migrants than had any of the other social workers. He eventually left the organization.

Because they find it difficult to work without an organizational base and equally difficult to work within the existing ones, many of the most concerned and active people drop out of migrant work altogether. For most social work activities are directed only toward making the migrant situation more bearable and not to changing it—films and old clothes are brought to the camps, women are trained to prepare surplus food and people are taught their rights *as migrants*. These activities are indeed important, but only help migrants adapt more efficiently to their present circumstances. Relatively few programs in the North are specifically directed toward training people for jobs out of the migrant labor stream. The experience of participants and observers alike in the study provides a strong indication that the invisibility of migrants is built into the very institutions created to deal with them.

Migrant invisibility is evident in the recruitment process itself. Arrangements for recruiting agricultural labor are handled through the farm labor division of the state employment services. For example, the grower makes his manpower needs known in the early spring and contracts are negotiated with crew leaders via the Farm Labor Service in Florida to transport a specified number of workers North on a specified date. Here the responsibility of the employment service and often the grower ends. The migrant himself is involved only when he is signed up by the crew leader, who acts as intermediary throughout the season. Growers provide camps and work sites, but many prefer to leave all dealings with the migrants themselves to the crew leaders. For example, 67 percent of 119 migrants interviewed had never been directly supervised by a grower. This avoidance of contact is often maintained at the expense of efficiency.

The crew leader system, developed from the delegation of employment responsibility, perpetuates migrant invisibility. It is the crew leader who assumes all responsibility, not only for recruitment and work supervision, but also for the sustenance of his crew, the policing of the camp, transportation and the provision of other services normally provided by a community. However, he is not accountable to outside authorities for these maintenance activities and may even have a stake in concealing how they are carried out—a point suggested by the threats made against farm workers who agree to testify before an investigating committee.

The desire of growers to minimize public awareness of their labor camps was apparent in the no trespassing signs found at the entrance of many camps, the difficulties encountered by VISTA volunteers who found themselves barred from some camps and problems in attempting to place students in camps for research purposes. One grower, who is in fact active on several migrant service committees, contends that the condition of migrants has greatly improved, but the problem now is that there are far too many social agencies involved. According to this grower, social workers do not recognize that migrants have different cultural backgrounds and that "they do not need the same things we do." From his perspective, most social work activities are destructive because they create unfavorable publicity. The growers' position is understandable in light of their vested interest in leaving things as they are. The subtle pervasiveness of this tendency is better illustrated by groups whose self-interest is less obvious.

Government inspectors are responsible for deciding whether or not migrant camps meet minimum standards. The main inspection occurs prior to the season, before the occupants of the camp arrive. Subsequent inspections, if they occur at all, are cursory. There are complex structural problems in the current system of inspection in New York State which hamper its effectiveness. The New York State Joint Legislative Committee Report in 1967 noted that local county health officers were not adequately enforcing the state sanitary code. "It is the opinion of this Committee that the County health officers and their assistants are too close to the leadership structure in the county, where the migrants are non-voters and have no representation in the power structure of these counties." As members of the local community, inspectors are often friends of growers and see them regularly the year round which may make it more difficult for them to enforce regulations. One inspector asserted in an interview that there was no exploitation in labor camps and that most migrants have too many expectations. He suggested that a large, self-contained labor camp be built with complete service facilities, including stores, clinics and child-care centers. This would avoid scattering people in tenant houses and small camps throughout agricultural communities. While such an arrangement might be convenient in terms of the availability of services, it is a solution that would further reduce migrant visibility.

Although enforcement problems are ubiquitous, legislation concerning labor camps places the burden of responsibility on the individual inspector. A content analysis of the New York State Health Code introduced in March 1968 reveals that in 16 items, the decision on the acceptability of a given condition is left to the discretion of the permit-issuing official. Other aspects of this legislation, intended to improve the situation, reveal an ignorance of the social realities in the camps and demonstrate the dangers of piecemeal improvement of a fundamentally poor situation. The vagueness of the earlier legislation had given the migrant a certain degree of independence from the crew leader. For example, because he was allowed to cook food in his room, he could avoid paying for prepared meals. Ironically, the new legislation, intended to improve fire safety, set minimum standards for cooking areas and left no alternative but to buy meals from the crew leader, thereby reinforcing his control. The intended solution of one problem only served to exacerbate another.

Camp conditions were the focus of a crisis that occurred when an organizer convinced a migrant to discuss the problems of farm labor on the radio. He described the decrepit buildings, the lack of sufficient water supply and the inadequate cooking and bathroom facilities. Despite the fact that the program was broadcast on an FM station with relatively few listeners, the publicity was sufficient to arouse not only local growers, but also community groups ostensibly concerned with improving just those conditions criticized. The next morning the grower, an inspector and the crew leader questioned the migrant who had appeared on the program and asked him to leave the camp. He went to town to rent a trailer, but later when he returned for his clothes, he was discouraged from leaving by the grower who feared further publicity.

One irate official at the government employment office complained that such publicity calls attention only to the worst camps, while ignoring all the positive changes in the migrant situation. The organizer, he felt, was interfering in what was none of his business. A church volunteer criticized the organizer, saying that he had angered a lot of people by intruding too aggressively; this would do more harm than good, for it would be damaging to social work programs in the area. The migrant who participated in the broadcast was spoken of with disdain ("he brought his own Beautyrest mattress North"), suggesting that he was not a real migrant because he showed concern for his own comfort.

A more serious incident revealed the extent and consequences of the invisibility of the migrant laborers. During the summer of 1966, a group of migrants in an agricultural community marched into town as a protest against their conditions, and fear of a riot was expressed. The event shocked community officials who had assumed that the migrants were well satisfied with the circumstances in which they lived. "Why," said the mayor, "they walked by here on the road and I waved to them and they laughed and smiled . . . real happy, you know." And the wife of the police chief noted, "this place is a paradise compared to what they are used to living in. Of course you or I wouldn't want to live that way, but I believe they like it fine."

Such a total lack of communication with the migrants is not entirely the fault of the community. The migrants themselves, as an outgroup subject to external pressures, control their visibility for purposes of protection in somewhat the same way as gypsies have developed subtle and complex mechanisms for maintaining a mystique of obscurity. Gypsies know back roads and inconspicuous gathering places, employ a private language and use decoys and facades such as fortune-telling; the latter diverts attention from what they consider to be the really important aspects of their culture. Invisibility permits autonomy and limits interference.

Migrants too are concerned primarily with self-protection. Living in the North for only part of the year and unfamiliar with many physical and social aspects of their environment, they feel isolated and alien. One articulate individual described his discomfort. In the South he knew where he could go and what he could do without getting into trouble; in the North he was never certain and he never knew what people were thinking. "Here people don't know where they stand and they are self-conscious all the time."

A second incentive for controlling visibility lies in the migrant's lack of autonomy. Control comes from outside the group and from such unpredictable sources as the weather and "the Man." Invisibility allows a sense of independence: "I don't drink. I mind my own business. It depends on how you act. If you're careful there'll be no trouble."

Finally, it is often pragmatically convenient to be invisible. Families needing income from their children's labor, for example, must be sensitive to their visibility when inspectors come to the fields.

Children working illegally often disappear from view as soon as state-government license plates are spotted. In one case, researchers using state vehicles found that their cars had to be relicensed or many people in the camps would disappear upon their arrival.

In many cases, crew leaders conceal overcrowded camp conditions. In one camp, approved for 86 occupants, there were 120 people, a discrepancy never noticed until a count was required for purposes of allocating government food during a time when there was no work. When the situation of overcrowding became visible, the crew leader with a logic clear only to himself eliminated 34 names, claiming that exactly 86 people were eligible. In effect he was able to make more than one-fourth of his crew disappear.

Certain aspects of migrant behavior correspond strikingly to the process of information control that Erving

Goffman has described as "stigma management." To maintain invisibility in Goffman's terms, it is necessary to avoid any action which might violate the expectations of others. This is an important group norm in migrant camps. There is considerable pressure to avoid arguing with a farmer or supervisor regardless of provocation. When one man spoke back to a farmer in a mildly facetious manner, he was immediately rebuked by the group for acting in this unexpected and therefore conspicuous fashion. Similarly, there are normative sanctions against picking too rapidly or too slowly. One must not stand out by working apart from the group and thereby possibly calling attention to the pace of others. Norms against ratebusting are of course not unique in this group, but they are particularly salient in this case because of the limited channels through which individuals may achieve mobility.

Similarly, group norms tend to level participants, to put down those who want to assume leadership. The outside society which perceives migrants as an undifferentiated group reinforces this leveling tendency and thus perpetuates stagnation.

Field researchers were struck by the dual personality exhibited by many migrants who assumed a meek demeanor in the presence of white people, but who were aggressive among their peers. To remain inconspicuous, these migrants had learned to assume different styles of behavior that meshed with the expectations of others. Thus, they manage the information that others receive about them.

A visitor to a migrant camp will often find himself next to a juke box turned up to full volume or faced with other means to limit communication, such as garbled accents, hand over mouth or silence. When not confronted directly, migrants maintain invisibility by simply avoiding outsiders.

Since there are few visitors, migrants remain unseen simply by staying in the camps. Certain people, primarily older workers, chose to stay out of town even when a ride was available. Younger people appeared less concerned, but when they did go to town they avoided unfamiliar areas. Once in the public eye, normative constraints against calling attention to the group were in operation. One young shoplifter was warned repeatedly, "don't cause trouble." Migrants hesitated to enter stores. In one case, a man who tried on a pair of shoes was afraid not to buy them. Although he did not want the shoes, he felt it would be less conspicuous to buy them than to leave without a purchase. A group of migrants on a truck being serviced at a garage would not ask for the key to the rest room, nor would they go into the station to buy soda.

The reluctance to call on outside authority is another symptom of the desire to maintain invisibility. Police are rarely requested to manage internal problems. Since migrants tend to distrust police authority, crew leaders prefer to maintain control themselves. When a police inquiry does take place, it is usually at the instigation of outsiders. For example, one man alienated several people in his camp and, afraid they would beat him, fled the camp. Local white residents who were concerned by his presence in their neighborhood initiated a police inquiry.

The police prefer to avoid involvement. A police officer, interviewed about his investigation of a fight between two migrants that occurred in the town, said that he instructed a group of migrants who had observed the fight to take care of the problem. "These are your people, you take care of them." They obliged by driving the men back to the camp. The officer claimed that he liked to avoid arresting migrants since it would keep them out of work. He preferred to ignore incidents and just to "quiet things down." Those migrants who do want police protection resent such an attitude, though they have come to expect it.

Migrant invisibility, then, is fostered both by the migrants themselves in an effort to adapt to their particular circumstances as well as by employers and social work groups and poverty organizations seeking to improve the situation. Groups seeking change share the preconception that while there are many problems, there are no alternatives to present arrangements. Solutions to problems are seen to lie in small, nonstructural changes. The primary concern is to avoid disturbing incidents which might in any way threaten the existing system. The tendency is to isolate migrants, to keep them in the camps where there is minimum visibility and limited contact with the outside community.

To render the migrant visible would expose the depths of the problem and certainly jeopardize the interests of those who have a stake in the system as it presently operates. Open acknowledgment of the existence of a social situation that is dissonant with basic social values would call these conditions into question. As long as the migrant remains out of sight, he is also out of mind. Disturbance may be minimized, but the obvious question remains: Can an invisible problem be resolved?

April 1972

FURTHER READING SUGGESTED BY THE AUTHOR:

Migrants, Sharecroppers and Mountaineers: Children of Crisis, Vol. II by Robert Coles (New York: Little Brown, 1972).

Migrants: Agricultural Workers in America's Northeast by William H. Friedland and Dorothy Nelkin (New York: Holt Rinehart & Winston, 1972).

Bibliography Relating to Agricultural Labor by David C. Ruesink
and T. Brice Batson (College Station, Texas: Texas
Agricultural Experiment Station, 1969).
Departmental Information Report Number 69-1.

On the Season by Dorothy Nelkin (Ithaca, New York:
New York State School of Industrial and Labor Relations,
Cornell University, 1970).

Life in Appalachia...
The Case of Hugh McCaslin

ROBERT COLES

Hugh McCaslin is unforgettable. He has red hair and, at 43, freckles. He stands six feet four. As he talked to me about his work in the coal mines, I kept wondering what he did with his height down inside the earth.

Once he must have been an unusually powerful man; even today his arms and legs are solid muscle. The fat he has added in recent years has collected in only one place, his waist, both front and back.

"I need some padding around my back; it's hurt, and I don't think it'll ever get back right. I broke it bad working, and they told me at first they'd have it fixed in no time flat, but they were wrong. I don't know if they were fooling themselves, or out to fool me in the bargain. It's hard to know *what's* going on around here—that's what I've discovered these last few years.

"I'll tell you, a man like me, he has a lot of time to think.

59

He'll sit around here, day upon day, and what else does he have to keep his mind on but his thoughts? I can't work, and even if I could, there's no work to do, not around here, no sir. They told me I'm 'totally incapacitated,' that's the words they used. They said my spine was hurt, and the nerves, and I can't walk and move about the way I should. As if I needed them to tell me!

"Then they gave me exercises and all, and told me I was lucky, because even though I wasn't in shape to go in the mines, I could do anything else, anything that's not too heavy. Sometimes I wonder what goes on in the heads of those doctors. They look you right in the eye, and they're wearing a straight face on, and they tell you you're sick, you've been hurt digging out coal, and you'll never be the same, but you're really not so bad off, because your back isn't so bad you can't be a judge, or a professor, or the president of the coal company or something like that, you know."

Once Hugh McCaslin (not his real name) asked me to look at an X-ray taken of his back and his shoulders—his vertebral column. He persuaded the company doctor to give him the X-ray, or so he said. (His wife told me that he had, in fact, persuaded the doctor's secretary to hand it over, and tell her boss—if he ever asked—that somehow the patient's "file" had been lost.) He was convinced that the doctor was a "company doctor"—which he assuredly was—and a "rotten, dishonest one." Anyway, what did *I* see in that X-ray? I told him that I saw very little. I am no radiologist, and whatever it was that ailed him could not be dramatically pointed out on an X-ray, or if it could I was not the man to do it. Well, yes he did know that, as a matter of fact:

"I got my nerves smashed down there in an accident.

I don't know about the bones. I think there was a lot of pressure, huge pressure on the nerves, and it affected the way I walk. The doctor said it wasn't a fracture on a big bone, just one near the spine. He said it wasn't 'too serious,' that I'd be O.K., just not able to go back to work, at least down there.

"Then, you see, they closed down the mine itself. That shows you I wasn't very lucky. My friends kept telling me I was lucky to be alive, and lucky to be through with it, being a miner. You know, we don't scare very easy. Together, we never would talk about getting hurt. I suppose it was somewhere in us, the worry; but the first time I heard my friends say anything like that was to me, not to themselves. They'd come by here when I was sick, and they'd tell me I sure was a fortunate guy, and God was smiling that day, and now He'd be smiling forever on me, because I was spared a *real* disaster, and it was bound to come, one day or another. It kind of got me feeling funny, hearing them talk like that *around my bed*, and then seeing them walk off real fast, with nothing to make *them* watch their step and take a pain pill every few hours.

"But after a while I thought maybe they did have something; and if I could just recover me a good pension from the company, and get my medical expenses all covered— well, then, I'd get better, as much as possible, and go fetch me a real honest-to-goodness job, where I could see the sun all day, and the sky outside, and breathe our air here, as much of it as I pleased, without a worry in the world.

"But that wasn't to be. I was dumb, real dumb, and hopeful. I saw them treating me in the hospital, and when they told me to go home I thought I was better, or soon would be. Instead, I had to get all kinds of treatments, and they said I'd have to pay for them, out of my savings or somewhere. And the pension I thought I was supposed to get, that was all in my mind, they said. They said the coal industry was going through a lot of changes, and you couldn't expect them to keep people going indefinitely, even if they weren't in the best of shape, even if it did happen down in the mines.

"Well, that's it, to make it short. I can't do hard work, and I have a lot of pain, every day of my life. I might be able to do light work, desk work, but hell, I'm not fit for anything like that; and even if I could, where's the work to be found? Around here? Never in a million years. We're doomed here, to sitting and growing the food we can and sharing our misery with one another.

"My brother, he helps; and my four sisters, they help; and my daddy, he's still alive and he can't help except to sympathize, and tell me it's a good thing I didn't get killed in that landslide and can see my boys grow up. He'll come over here and we start drinking. You bet, he's near 80, and we start drinking, and remembering. My daddy will ask me if I can recollect the time I said I'd save a thousand dollars for myself by getting a job in the mines and I say I sure can, and can he recollect the time he said I'd better not get too greedy, because there's bad that comes with good in this world, and especially way down there inside the earth."

He will take a beer or two and then get increasingly angry. His hair seems to look wilder, perhaps because he puts his hands through it as he talks. His wife becomes nervous and tries to give him some bread or crackers, and he becomes sullen or embarrassingly direct with her. She is trying to "soak up" his beer. She won't even let it hit his stomach and stay there a while. She wants it back. He tells her, "Why don't you *keep* your beer, if you won't let it do a thing for me?"

They have five sons, all born within nine years. The oldest is in high school and dreams of the day he will join the army. He says he will be "taken" in, say, in Charleston or Beckley—in his mind, any "big city" will do. He will be sent off to California or Florida or "maybe New York" for basic training; eventually he will "land himself an assignment— anywhere that's good, and it'll be far away from here, I do believe that." Hugh McCaslin becomes enraged when he hears his son talk like that; with a few beers in him he becomes especially enraged:

"That's the way it is around here. That's what's hap- pened to us. That's what they did to us. They made us lose any honor we had. They turned us idle. They turned us into a lot of grazing sheep, lucky to find a bit of pasture here and there. We don't *do* anything here any- more; and so my boys, they'll all want to leave, and they will. But they'll want to come back, too—because this land, it's in their bones going way back, and you don't shake off your ancestors that easy, no sir.

"My daddy, he was born right up the road in this here hollow, and his daddy, and back to a long time ago. There isn't anyone around here we're not kin to somehow, near or far. My daddy was the one supposed to leave for the mines. He figured he could make more money than he could dream about, and it wasn't too far to go. He went for a while, but some years later he quit. He couldn't take it. I grew up in a camp near the mine, and I'd still be there if it wasn't that I got hurt and moved back here to the hollow. Even while we were at the camp we used to come back here on Sundays, I remember, just like now they come here on weekends from Cincinnati and Dayton and those places, and even from way off in Chicago. I can recall the car we got; everybody talked about it, and when we'd drive as near here as we could—well, the people would come, my grandparents and all my uncles and aunts and cousins, and they'd look and look at that Ford, before they'd see if it was *us,* and say hello to us. I can recollect in my mind being shamed and wanting to disappear in one of those pockets, where my daddy would keep his pipes. My mother would say it wasn't they didn't want to see us, but the Ford, it was real special to them, and could you blame them for not looking at us?

"That was when things were really good. Except that even then I don't think we were all that contented. My mother always worried. Every day, come 3 or so in the afternoon, I could tell she was starting to worry. Will anything happen? Will he get hurt? Will they be coming over soon, to give me some bad news? (No, we had no telephone, and neither did the neighbors.) It got so we'd come home from school around 2 or so, and just sit there with her, pretending—pretending to do things, and say things. And then he'd come in, every time. We could hear his voice coming, or his steps, or the door, and we'd all loosen up—and pretend again, that there was nothing we'd worry about, because there wasn't nothing *to* worry about.

"One day—I think I was seven or eight, because I was in school, I know that—we had a bad scare. Someone came to the school and told the teacher something, whispered it in her ear. She turned into a sheet, and she looked as though she'd start crying. The older kids knew what had happened, just from her looks. (Yes, it was a one-room schoolhouse, just like the one we have here, only a little bigger.) They ran out, and she almost took off after them, except for the fact that she remembered us. So she turned around and told us there that something bad had happened down in the mines, an explosion, and we should go home and wait there, and if our mothers weren't there—well, wait until they got home.

"But we wanted to go with her. Looking back at it, I think she worried us. So she decided to take us, the little ones. And I'll tell you, I can remember that walk with her like it was just today. I can see it, and I can tell you what she said, and what we did, and all. We walked and walked, and then we came through the woods and there they were, all of a sudden before our eyes. The people there, just standing around and almost nothing being said between them. It was so silent I thought they'd all turn around and see us, making noise. But, you see, we must have stopped talking, too, because for a while they didn't even give us a look over their shoulders. Then we come closer, and I could hear there was noise after all: The women were crying, and there'd be a cough or something from some of the miners.

"That's what sticks with you, the miners wondering if their buddies were dead or alive down there. Suddenly I saw my father, and my mother. They were with their arms about one another—real unusual—and they were waiting, like the rest.

"Oh, we got home that night, yes, and my daddy said they were gone—they were dead and we were going away. And we did. The next week we drove here in our Ford, and I can hear my daddy saying it wasn't worth it, money and a car, if you die young, or you live but your lungs get poisoned, and all that, and you never see the sun except on Sundays.

"But what choice did he have? And what choice did I have? I thought I might want to do some farming, like my grandfather, but there's no need for me, and my grandfather couldn't really keep more than himself going, I mean with some food and all. Then I thought it'd be nice to finish school, and maybe get a job someplace near, in a town not a big city. But everything was collapsing all over the country then, and you'd be crazy to think you were going to get anything by leaving here and going out there, with the lines standing for soup—oh yes, we heard on the radio what it was like all over.

"It could be worse, you say to yourself, and you resolve to follow your daddy and be a miner. That's what I did. He said we had a lousy day's work, but we got good pay, and we could buy things. My daddy had been the richest man in his family for a while. In fact, he was the only man in his family who had any money at all. After the family looked over our Ford, they'd give us that real tired and sorry look, as though they needed some help real bad, and that's when my daddy would hand out the dollar bills, one after the other. I can picture it right now. You feel rich, and you feel real kind."

Hugh McCaslin's life wouldn't be that much better even if he had not been seriously hurt in a mine accident. The miners who were his closest friends are now unemployed, almost every one of them. They do not feel cheated out of a disability pension, but for all practical purposes he and they are equally idle, equally bitter, equally sad. With no prompting from my psychiatric mind he once put it this way:

"They talk about depressions in this country. I used to hear my daddy talk about them all the time, depressions. It wasn't so bad for my daddy and me in the thirties, when the Big One, the Big Depression, was knocking everyone down, left and right. He had a job, and I knew I was going to have one as soon as I was ready, and I did. Then when the war come, they even kept me home. They said we were keeping everything going over here in West Virginia. You can't run factories without coal. I felt I wouldn't mind going, and getting a look at things out there, but I was just as glad to stay here, I guess. I was married, and we were starting with the kids, so it would have been hard. My young brother, he went. He wasn't yet a miner, and they just took him when he was 18, I think. He come back here and decided to stay out of the mines, but it didn't make much difference in the end, anyway. We're all out of the mines now around here.

"So, you see it's *now* that *we're* in a depression. They say things are pretty good in most parts of the country, from what you see on TV, but not so here. We're in the biggest depression ever here: We have no money, and no welfare payments, and we're expected to scrape by like dogs. It gets to your mind after a while. You feel as low as can be, and nervous about everything. That's what a depression does, makes you dead broke, with a lot of bills and the lowest spirits you can ever picture a man having. Sometimes I get up and I'm ready to go over to an under-taker and tell him to do something with me real fast."

I have spent days and nights with the McCaslin family, and Hugh McCaslin doesn't always feel that "low," that depressed, that finished with life. I sup-pose it can be said that he has "adapted" to the hard, miserable life he faces. At times he shouts and screams about "things," and perhaps in that way keeps himself explicitly angry rather than sullen and brooding. His friends call him a "firebrand," and blame his temper on his red hair. In fact, he says what they are thinking, and need to hear said by someone. They come to see him, and in Mrs. Mc-Caslin's words, "get him going." They bring him home-made liquor to help matters along.

The McCaslins are early risers, but no one gets up earlier than the father. He suffers pain at night; his back and his legs hurt. He has been told that a new hard mattress would help, and hot baths, and aspirin. He spends a good part of the night awake —"thinking and dozing off and then coming to, real sudden-like, with a pain here or there." For a while he thought of sleeping on the floor, or trying to get another bed, but he could not bear the prospect of being alone:

"My wife, Margaret, has kept me alive. She has some

of God's patience in her, that's the only way I figure she's been able to last it. She smiles when things are so dark you'd think the end has come. She soothes me, and tells me it'll get better, and even though I know it won't I believe her for a few minutes, and that helps."

So he tosses and turns in their bed, and his wife has learned to sleep soundly but to wake up promptly when her husband is in real pain. They have aspirin and treat it as something special—and expensive. I think Hugh McCaslin realizes that he suffers from many different kinds of pain; perhaps if he had more money he might have been addicted to all sorts of pain-killers long ago. Certainly when I worked in a hospital I saw patients like him—hurt and in pain, but not "sick" enough to require hospitalization, and in fact "chronically semi-invalids." On the other hand, such patients had tried and failed at any number of jobs. We will never know how Hugh McCaslin might have felt today if he had found suitable work after his accident, or had received further medical care. Work is something a patient needs as he starts getting better, as anyone who works in a "rehabilitation unit" of a hospital well knows. Hugh McCaslin lacked medical care when he needed it, lacks it today, and in his own words needs a "time-killer" as much as a pain-killer. His friends despair, drink, "loaf about," pick up a thing here and there to do, and "waste time real efficiently." So does he—among other things, by dwelling on his injured body.

He dwells on his children, too. There are five of them, and he wants all of them to leave West Virginia. Sometimes in the early morning, before his wife is up, he leaves bed to look at them sleeping:

"I need some hope, and they have it, in their young age and the future they have, if they only get the hell out of here before it's too late. Oh, I like it here, too. It's pretty, and all that. It's peaceful. I'm proud of us people. We've been here a long time, and we needed real guts to stay and last. And who wants to live in a big city? I've been in some of our cities, here in West Virginia, and they're no big value, from what I can see, not so far as bringing up a family. You have no land, no privacy, a lot of noise, and all that. But if it's between living and dying, I'll take living; and right here, right now, I think we're dying—dying away, slow but sure, every year more and more so."

He worries about his children in front of them. When they get up they see him sitting and drinking coffee in the kitchen. He is wide-awake, and hungrier for company than he knows. He wants to learn what they'll be doing that day. He wants to talk about things, about the day's events and inevitably a longer span of time, the future: "Take each day like your life hangs on it. That's being young, when you can do that, when you're not trapped and have some choice on things." The children are drowsy, but respectful. They go about dressing and taking coffee and doughnuts with him. They are as solicitous as he is. Can they make more coffee? They ask if they can bring him anything—even though they know full well his answer: "No, just yourselves."

Mrs. McCaslin may run the house, but she makes a point of checking every decision with her husband.

He "passes on" even small matters—something connected with one of the children's schoolwork, or a neighbor's coming visit, or a project for the church. She is not sly and devious; not clever at appearing weak but "manipulating" all the while. She genuinely defers to her husband, and his weakness, his illness, his inability to find work—and none of those new medical, social, or psychological "developments" have made her see fit to change her ways. Nor is he inclined to sit back and let the world take *everything* out of his hands. As a matter of fact, it is interesting to see how assertive a man and a father he still is, no matter how awful his fate continues to be. He is *there,* and always there—in spirit as well as in body. I have to compare him not only with certain Negro fathers I know, who hide from welfare workers and flee their wives and children in fear and shame and anger, but also with a wide range of white middle-class fathers who maintain a round-the-clock absence from home (for business reasons, for "social" reasons), or else demonstrate a much-advertised "passivity" while there. Hugh McCaslin, as poor as one can be in America, not at all well-educated, jobless, an invalid, and a worried, troubled man, nevertheless exerts a strong and continuing influence upon everyone in his family. He is, again, *there*—not just at home, but very much involved in almost everything his wife and children do. He talks a lot. He has strong ideas, and he has a temper. He takes an interest in all sorts of problems—not only in those that plague Road's Bend Hollow:

"My daddy was a great talker. He wasn't taken in by

the big people who run this country. He didn't read much, even then when he was young, but he had his beliefs. He said we don't give everyone a break here, and that's against the whole purpose of the country, when it was first settled. You know, there are plenty of people like him. They know how hard it is for a working man to get his share—to get *anything*. Let me tell you, if we had a chance, men like me, we'd vote for a different way of doing things. It just isn't right to use people like they're so much dirt, hire them and fire them and give them no respect and no real security. A few make fortunes and, the rest of us, we're lucky to have our meals from day to day. That's not right; it just isn't.

"I tell my boys not to be fooled. It's tough out there in the world, and it's tough here, too. We've got little here except ourselves. They came in here, the big companies, and bled us dry. They took everything, our coal, our land, our trees, our health. We died like we were in a war, fighting for those companies—and we were lucky to get enough money to bury our kin. They tell me sometimes I'm bitter, my brothers do, but they're just as bitter as I am—they don't talk as much, that's the only difference. Of course it got better here with unions and with some protection the workers got through the government. But you can't protect a man when the company decides to pull out; when it says it's got all it can get, so goodbye folks, and take care of yourselves, because we're moving on to some other place, and we just can't do much more than tell you it was great while it lasted, and you helped us out a lot, yes sir you did."

He does not always talk like that. He can be quiet for long stretches of time, obviously and moodily quiet. His wife finds his silences hard to bear. She doesn't know what they will "lead to." Every day she asks her husband whether there is anything "special" he wants to eat—even though they both know there isn't much they can afford but the daily mainstays—bread, coffee, doughnuts, crackers, some thin stew, potatoes, homemade jam, biscuits. Mrs. McCaslin defers to her husband, though; one way is to pay him the courtesy of asking him what he wants. I have often heard them go back and forth about food, and as if for all the world they were far better off, with more choices before them:

"Anything special you want for supper?"

"No. Anything suits me fine. I'm not too hungry."

"Well, if that's it then I'd better make you hungry with something special."

"What can do that?"

"I thought I'd fry up the potatoes real good tonight and cut in some onions. It's better than boiling, and I've got some good pork to throw in. You wait and see."

"I will. It sounds good."

He hurts and she aches for him. His back has its "bad spells," and she claims her own back can "feel the pain that goes through his." They don't touch each other very much in a stranger's presence, or even, I gather, before their children, but they give each other long looks of recognition, sympathy, affection, and sometimes anger or worse. They understand each other in that silent, real, lasting way that defies the gross labels that I and my kind call upon. It is hard to convey in words—theirs or mine—the subtle, delicate, largely unspoken, and continual *sense of each other* (that is the best that I can do) that they have. In a gesture, a glance, a frown, a smile they talk and agree and disagree:

"I can tell what the day will be like for Hugh when he first gets up. It's all in how he gets out of bed, slow or with a jump to it. You might say we all have our good days and bad ones, but Hugh has a lot of time to give over to his moods, and around here I guess we're emotional, you might say."

I told her that I thought an outsider like me might not see it that way. She wanted to know what I meant, and I told her: "They call people up in the hollow 'quiet,' and they say they don't show their feelings too much, to each other, let alone in front of someone like me."

"Well, I don't know about that," she answered quickly, a bit piqued. "I don't know what reason they have for that. Maybe they don't have good ears. We don't talk *loud* around here, but we say what's on our mind, straightaway, I believe. I never was one for mincing on words, and I'll tell anyone what's on my mind, be he from around here or way over on the other side of the world. I do believe we're cautious here, and we give a man every break we can, because you don't have it easy around here, no matter who you are; so maybe that's why they think we're not given to getting excited and such. But we do."

I went back to Hugh. Did she think he was more "emotional" than others living nearby?

"Well, I'd say it's hard to say. He has a temper, but I think that goes for all his friends. I think he's about ordinary, only because of his sickness he's likely to feel bad more than some, and it comes out in his moods. You know, when we were married he was the most cheerful man I'd ever met. I mean he smiled all the time, not just because someone said something funny. His daddy told me I was getting the happiest of his kids, and I told him I believed he was right, because I'd already seen it for myself. Today he's his old self sometimes, and I almost don't want to see it, because it makes me think back and remember the good times we had.

"Oh, we have good times now, too; don't mistake me. They just come rare, compared to when times were good. And always it's his pain that hangs over us; we never know when he'll be feeling right, from day to day.

"But when he's got his strength and there's nothing ailing him, he's all set to work, and it gets bad trying to figure what he might do. We talk of moving, but we ask ourselves where we'd go to. We don't want to travel a thousand miles only to be lost in some big city and not have even what we've got. Here there's a neighbor, and our kin, always. We have the house, and we manage to scrape things together, and no one of my kids has ever starved to death. They don't get the food they should, sometimes, but they eat, and they like what I do with food. In fact they complain at church. They say others don't brown the potatoes enough, or the biscuits. And they like a good chocolate cake, and I have that as often as I can.

"When Hugh is low-down he doesn't want to get out of bed, but I make him. He'll sit around and not do much. Every few minutes he'll call my name, but then he won't really have much to say. I have those aspirin, but you can't really afford to use them all the time.

"When he feels good, though, he'll go do chores. He'll make sure we have plenty of water, and he'll cut away some wood and lay it up nearby. He'll walk up the road and see people. He has friends, you know, who aren't sick like him, but it doesn't do them much good around here to be healthy. They can't work any more than Hugh can. It's bad, all the time bad.

"We find our own work, though, and we get paid in the satisfaction you get. We try to keep the house in good shape, and we keep the road clear all year round. That can be a job come winter.

"A lot of the time Hugh says he wished he could read better. He'll get an old magazine—the Reader's Digest, or the paper from Charleston—and he'll stay with it for hours. I can see he's having a tough time, but it keeps him busy. He tells the kids to remember his mistakes and not to make them all over again. Then they want to know why he made them. And we're off again. He talks about the coal companies and how they bribed us out of our 'souls,' and how he was a fool, and how it's different now. When they ask what they'll be doing with their reading and writing, it's hard to give them an answer without telling them to move. You don't want to do that, but maybe you do, too. I don't know.

"Hugh fought the television. He said it was no good, and we surely didn't have the money to get one. You can get them real cheap, though, secondhand, and there's a chance to learn how to fix it yourself, because some of the men who come back from the army, they've learned how and they'll teach you and do it for you if you ask them. We had to get one, finally. The kids, they said everyone else didn't have the money, any more than we did, but somehow they got the sets, so why couldn't we? That started something, all right. Hugh wanted to know if they thought we could manufacture money. So they wanted to know how the others got their sets. And Hugh said he didn't know, but if they would go find out, and come tell him, why then he'd show them that each family is different, and you can't compare people like that. Well, then they mentioned it to their uncle—he works down there in the school, keeping it in order, and he's on a regular salary, you know, and lives as good as anyone around here, all things told, I'd say. So he came and told us he'd do it, get a set for us, because the kids really need them. They feel left out without TV.

"That got Hugh going real bad. He didn't see why the radio wasn't enough, and he wasn't going to take and take and take. He wanted help, but not for a TV set. And then he'd get going on the coal companies, and how we got that radio for cash, and it was brand-new and expensive, but he was making plenty of money then. And he didn't want to go begging, even from kin. And we could just do without, so long as we eat and have a place to sleep and no one's at our door trying to drive us away or take us to jail.

"Finally I had to say something. I had to. It was one of the hardest things I've ever had to do. He was getting worse and worse, and the kids they began to think he was wrong in the head over a thing like TV, and they didn't know why; they couldn't figure it out. He said they wouldn't see anything but a lot of trash, and why should we let it all come in here like that? And he said they'd lose interest in school, and become hypnotized or something, and he'd read someplace it happens. And he said gadgets and machines, they came cheap, but you end up losing a lot more than you get, and that was what's happening in America today.

"Now, the kids could listen for so long, and they're respectful to him, to both of us, I think you'll agree. They'd try to answer him, real quiet, and say it wasn't so important, TV wasn't, it was just there to look at, and we would all do it and have a good time. And everyone was having it, but that didn't mean that the world was changing, or that you'd lose anything just because you looked at a picture every once in a while.

"And finally, as I say, I joined in. I had to—and I sided with them. I said they weren't going to spend their lives looking at TV, no sir, but it would be O.K. with me if we had it in the house, that I could live with it, and I think we could all live with it. And Hugh, he just looked at me and didn't say another word, not that day or any other afterwards until much later on, when we had the set already, and he would look at the news and listen real careful to what they tell you might be happening. He told me one day, it was a foolish fight we all had, and television wasn't any better or worse than a lot of other things. But he wished the country would make more than cheap TVs. 'We could all live without TV if we had something more to look forward to,' he said. I couldn't say anything back. He just wasn't feeling good that day, and to tell the truth TV is good for him when he's like that, regardless of what he says. He watches it like he used to listen to his radio, and he likes it better than he'd ever admit to himself, I'm sure."

On Sundays they go to church. Hugh says he doesn't much believe in "anything," but he goes; he stays home only when he doesn't feel good, not out of any objection to prayer. They all have their Sunday clothes, and they all enjoy getting into them. They become new and different people. They walk together down the hollow and along the road that takes them to a Baptist church. They worship vigorously and sincerely, and with a mixture of awe, bravado, passion, and restraint that leaves an outside observer feeling, well—skeptical, envious, surprised, mystified, admiring, and vaguely nostalgic. I think they emerge much stronger and more united for the experience, and with as much "perspective," I suppose, as others get from different forms of contemplation, submission, and joint participation. Hugh can be as stoical as anyone else, and in church his stoicism can simply pour out. The world *is* confusing, you see. People have *always* suffered, good people. Somewhere, somehow, it is not all for naught—but that doesn't mean one should raise one's hopes too high, not on this earth.

After church there is "socializing," and its importance need not be stressed in our self-conscious age of "groups" that solve "problems" or merely facilitate "interaction." When I have asked myself what "goes on" in those "coffee periods," I remind myself that I heard a lot of people laughing, exchanging news, offering greetings, expressing wishes, fears, congratulations and condolences. I think there is a particular warmth and intensity to some of the meetings because, after all, people do not see much of one another during the week. Yet how many residents of our cities or our suburbs see one another as regularly as these "isolated" people do? Hugh McCaslin put it quite forcefully: "We may not see much of anyone for a few days, but Sunday will come and we see everyone we want to see, and by the time we go home we know everything there is to know." As some of us say, they "communicate efficiently."

There is, I think, a certain hunger for companionship that builds up even among people who do not feel as "solitary" as some of their observers have considered them. Particularly at night one feels the woods and the hills close in on "the world." The McCaslins live high up in a hollow, but they don't have a "view." Trees tower over their cabin, and the smoke rising from their chimney has no space at all to dominate. When dusk comes there are no lights to be seen, only their lights to turn on. In winter they eat at about 5 and they are in bed about 7:30 or 8. The last hour before bed is an almost formal time. Every evening Mr. McCaslin smokes his pipe and either reads or carves wood. Mrs. McCaslin has finished putting things away after supper and sits sewing—"mending things and fixing things;

there isn't a day goes by that something doesn't tear." The children watch television. They have done what homework they have (or are willing to do) before supper. I have never heard them reprimanded for failing to study. Their parents tell them to go to school; to stay in school; to do well in school—but they aren't exactly sure it makes much difference. They ask the young to study, but I believe it is against their "beliefs" to say one thing and mean another, to children or anyone else.

In a sense, then, they are blunt and truthful with each other. They say what they think, but worry about how to say what they think so that the listener remains a friend or—rather often—a friendly relative. Before going to bed they say good-night, and one can almost feel the reassurance that goes with the greeting. It is very silent "out there" or "outside."

"Yes, I think we have good manners," Hugh McCaslin once told me. "It's a tradition, I guess, and goes back to Scotland, or so my daddy told me. I tell the kids that they'll know a lot more than I do when they grow up, or I hope they will; but I don't believe they'll have more consideration for people—no sir. We teach them to say hello in the morning, to say good morning, like you said. I know it may not be necessary, but it's good for people living real close to be respectful of one another. And the same goes for the evening.

"Now, there'll be fights. You've seen us take after one another. That's O.K. But we settle things on the same day, and we try not to carry grudges. How can you carry a grudge when you're just this one family here, and miles away from the next one? Oh, I know it's natural to be spiteful and carry a grudge. But you can only carry it so far, that's what I say. Carry it until the sun goes down, then wipe the slate clean and get ready for another day. I say that a lot to the kids."

Once I went with the McCaslins to a funeral. A great-uncle of Mrs. McCaslin's had died at 72. He happened to be a favorite of hers and of her mother. They lived much nearer to a town than the McCaslins do, and were rather well-to-do. He had worked for the county government all his life—in the Appalachian region, no small position. The body lay at rest in a small church, with hand-picked flowers in bunches around it. A real clan had gathered from all over, as well as friends. Of course it was a sad occasion, despite the man's advanced age; yet even so I was struck by the restraint of the people, their politeness to one another, no matter how close or "near kin" they were. For a moment I watched them move about and tried to block off their subdued talk from my brain. It occurred to me that, were they dressed differently and in a large manor home, they might very much resemble English gentry at a reception. They were courtly people; they looked it and acted it. Many were tall, thin, and close-mouthed. A few were potbellied, as indeed befits a good lusty duke or duchess. They could smile and even break out into a laugh, but it was always noticeable when it happened. In general they were not exactly demonstrative or talkative, yet they were clearly interested in one another and had very definite and strong sentiments, feelings, emotions, whatever. In other words, as befits the gentry, they had feelings but had them under "appropriate" control.

They also seemed suitably resigned, or philosophical —as the circumstances warranted. What crying there was, had already been done. There were no outbursts of any kind, and no joviality either. It was not a wake.

A few days later Hugh McCaslin of Road's Bend Hollow talked about the funeral and life and death:

"He probably went too early, from what I hear. He was in good health, and around here you either die very young —for lack of a doctor—or you really last long. That's the rule, though I admit we have people live to all ages, like being sick as I am. It happens to you, and you know it, but that's O.K. When I was a boy I recall my people burying their old people, right near where we lived. We had a little graveyard, and we used to know all our dead people pretty well. You know, we'd play near their graves, and go ask our mother or daddy about who this one was and what he did, and like that. The other way was through the Bible: Everything was written down on pieces of paper inside the family Bible. There'd be births and marriages and deaths, going way back, I guess as far back as the beginning of the country. I'm not sure of the exact time, but a couple of hundred years, easy.

"We don't do that now—it's probably one of the biggest changes, maybe. I mean apart from television and things like that. We're still religious, but we don't keep the records, and we don't bury our dead nearby. It's just not that much of a *home* here, a place that you have and your kin always had and your children and theirs will have, until the end of time, when God calls us all to account. This here place—it's a good house, mind you—but it's just a place I got. A neighbor of my daddy's had it, and he left it, and my daddy heard and I came and fixed it up and we have it for nothing. We worked hard and put a lot into it, and we treasure it, but it never was a *home,* not the kind I knew, and my wife did. We came back to the hollow, but it wasn't like it used to be when we were kids and you felt you were living in the same place all your ancestors did. We're *part* of this land, we were here to start and we'll probably see it die, me or my kids will, the way things are going. There will be no one left here and the stripminers will kill every good acre we have. I thought of that at the funeral. I thought maybe it's just as well to die now, if everything's headed in that direction. I guess that's what happens at a funeral. You get to thinking."

June 1968

FURTHER READING SUGGESTED BY THE AUTHOR:

Night Comes to the Cumberland by Harry M. Caudill (Boston: Little, Brown & Co., 1963). A first-rate general historical account of the problems that plague Appalachia; probably the best known contemporary work.

Stinking Creek by John Fetterman (New York: E. P. Dutton & Co., 1967). A careful description of one hollow, sensitively done with great candor and honesty.

Yesterday's People by Jack A. Weller (Lexington, Ky.: University of Kentucky Press, 1965). A minister's social and cultural observations, along with some accurate, thoughtful, and properly ambiguous conclusions.

In the Valley
of the Shadows: Kentucky

BRUCE JACKSON

Along the roadsides and in backyards are the cannibalized cadavers of old cars: there is no other place to dump them, there are no junkyards that have any reason to haul them away. Streambeds are littered with old tires, cans, pieces of metal and plastic. On a sunny day the streams and creeks glisten with pretty blue spots from the Maxwell House coffee tins and Royal Crown Cola cans. For some reason the paint used by Maxwell House and Royal Crown doesn't wear off very quickly, and while the paint and paper on other cans are peeling to reveal an undistinctive aluminum color, the accumulating blues of those two brands make for a most peculiar local feature.

Winter in eastern Kentucky is not very pretty. In some places you see the gouged hillsides where the strip and auger mines have ripped away tons of dirt and rock to get at the mineral seams underneath; below the gouges you see the littered valleys where the overburden, the earth they have ripped and scooped away, has been dumped in spoil banks. The streams stink from the augerholes' sulfurous exudations; the hillsides no longer hold water back because the few trees and bushes are small and thin, so there is continual erosion varying the ugliness in color only.

Most of the people around here live outside the town in hollows and along the creeks. Things are narrow: the hills rise up closely and flatland is at a premium. A residential area will stretch out for several miles, one or two houses and a road thick, with hills starting up just behind the outhouse. Sometimes, driving along the highway following the Big Sandy river, there is so little flat space that the highway is on one side of the river and the line of houses is on the other, with plank suspension bridges every few miles connecting the two. Everything is crushed together. You may ride five miles without passing a building, then come upon a half-dozen houses, each within ten feet of its neighbor. And churches: the Old Regular Baptist church, the Freewill Baptist church, the Meta Baptist church. On the slopes of the hills are cemeteries, all neatly tended; some are large and old, some have only one or two recent graves in them.

In winter, when the sun never rises very far above the horizon, the valley floors get only about four hours of direct sunlight a day; most of the days are cloudy anyhow. One always moves in shadow, in greyness. Children grow up without ever seeing the sun rise or set.

The day of the company store and company house is gone. So are most of the big companies around here. This is small truck mine country now, and operators of the small mines don't find stores and houses worth their time. The old company houses worth living in have been bought up, either as rental property or for the new owner's personal use; the company houses still standing but not worth living in comprise the county's only public housing for the very poor.

At the end of one of the hollows running off Marrow-bone Creek, three miles up a road you couldn't make, even in dry weather, without four-wheel drive, stands an old cabin. It is a log cabin, but there is about it nothing romantic or frontiersy, only grimness. Scratched in the kitchen window, by some unknown adult or child, are the crude letters of the word victory. Over what or whom we don't know. It is unlikely anyway. There are no victories here, only occasional survivors, and if survival is a victory it is a mean and brutal one.

Inside the cabin a Barbie doll stands over a nearly opaque mirror in a room lighted by a single bare 60-watt bulb. In the middle of the room a coal stove spews outrageous amounts of heat. When the stove is empty the room is cold and damp. There is no middle area of comfort. The corrugated cardboard lining the walls doesn't stop drafts very well and most of the outside chinking is gone. On one side of the room with the stove is the entrance to the other bedroom, on the other side is the kitchen. There ar no doors inside the house. A woman lives here with her nine children.

If all the nine children were given perfectly balanced full meals three times a day from now on, still some of them would never be well. A 15-year-old daughter loses patches of skin because of an irreversible vitamin deficiency, and sometimes, because of the supporations and congealing, they have to soak her clothing off when she comes home from school. Last month the baby was spitting up blood for a while but that seems to have stopped.

It might be possible to do something for the younger ones, but it is not likely anyone will. The husband went somewhere and didn't come back; that was over a year ago.

The welfare inspector came a few months ago and found out that someone had given the family a box of clothes for the winter; the welfare check was cut by $20 a month after that. When the woman has $82 she can get $120 worth of food stamps; if she doesn't have the $82, she gets no food stamps at all. For a year, the entire family had nothing for dinner but one quart of green beans each night. Breakfast was fried flour and coffee. A friend told me the boy said he had had meat at a neighbor's house once.

This is Pike County, Kentucky. It juts like a chipped arrowhead into the bony hill country of neighboring West Virginia. Pike County has about 70,000 residents and, the Chamber of Commerce advertises, it produces more coal than any other county in the world. The county seat, Pikeville, has about 6,000 residents; it is the only real town for about 30 miles.

The biggest and bitterest event in Pike County's past was sometime in the 1880s when Tolbert McCoy killed Big Ellison Hatfield: it started a feud that resulted in 65 killed, settled nothing and wasn't won by either side. The biggest and bitterest thing in recent years has been the War on Poverty: it doesn't seem to have killed anyone, but it hasn't settled anything or won any major battles either.

About 7,500 men are employed by Pike County's mines: 1,000 drive trucks, five hundred work at the tipples (the docks where coal is loaded into railway cars) and mine offices, and 6,000 work inside. Most of the mines are small and it doesn't take very many men to work them: an automated truck mine can be handled by about eight men. Some people work at service activities: they pump gas, sell shoes, negotiate contracts (there are about 40 lawyers in this little town), dispense drugs, direct traffic, embalm—all those things that make an American town go. There are six industrial firms in the area; two of them are beverage companies, one is a lumber company; the total employment of the six firms is 122 men and women.

A union mine pays $28-$38 per day, with various benefits, but few of the mines in Pike County are unionized. The truck mines, where almost all the men work, pay $14 per day, with almost no benefits. The United Mine Workers of America were strong here once, but when times got hard the union let a lot of people down and left a lot of bitterness behind. Not only did the union make deals with the larger companies that resulted in many of its own men being thrown out of work (one of those deals recently resulted in a $7.3 million conspiracy judgment against the UMWA and Consolidation Coal Company), but it made the abandonment complete by lifting the unemployed workers' medical cards and shutting down the union hospitals in the area. For most of the area, those cards and hospitals were the only source of medical treatment. There has been talk of organizing the truck mines and someone told me the UMW local was importing an old-time firebreathing organizer to get things going, but it doesn't seem likely the men will put their lives on the line another time.

With Frederic J. Fleron, Jr., an old friend then on the faculty of the University of Kentucky in Lexington, I went to visit Robert Holcomb, president of the Independent Coal Operator's Association, president of the Chamber of Commerce and one of the people in the county most vocally at war with the poverty program. His office door was decorated with several titles: Dixie Mining Co., Roberts Engineering Co., Robert Holcomb and Co., Chloe Gas Co., Big Sandy Coal Co. and Martha Collieries, Inc.

One of the secretaries stared at my beard as if it were a second nose; she soon got control of herself and took us in to see Holcomb. (Someone had said to me the day before,

"Man, when Holcomb sees you with that beard on he's gonna be sure you're a communist." "What if I tell him I'm playing Henry the Fifth in a play at the university?" "Then he'll be sure Henry the Fifth is a communist too.") Holcomb took the beard better than the girl had: his expression remained nicely neutral. He offered us coffee and introduced us to his partner, a Mr. Roberts, who sat in a desk directly opposite him. On the wall behind Roberts' head was a large white flying map of the United States with a brownish smear running over Louisiana, Mississippi and most of Texas; the darkest splotch was directly over New Orleans. The phone rang and Roberts took the call; he tilted back in his chair, his head against New Orleans and Lake Pontchartrain.

Holcomb was happy to talk about his objections to the poverty program. "I'm a firm believer that you don't help a man by giving him bread unless you give him hope for the future, and poverty programs have given them bread only." The problem with the Appalachian Volunteers (an anti-poverty organization partially funded by OEO, now pretty much defunct) was "they got no supervision. They brought a bunch of young people in, turned 'em loose and said, 'Do your thing.' . . . I think they have created a disservice rather than a service by creating a lot of disillusionment by making people expect things that just can't happen."

He told us something about what was happening. The coal industry had been expanding rapidly. "Over the last eight years the truck mining industry has created an average of 500 new jobs a year." He sat back. "We're working to bring the things in here that will relieve the poverty permanently." He talked of bringing other kinds of industry to the area and told us about the incentives they were offering companies that were willing to relocate. "We know a lot of our people are not fitted for mining," he said.

(It is not just a matter of being "fitted" of course. There

is the problem of those who are wrecked by silicosis and black lung who can do nothing but hope their doctor bills won't go up so much they'll have to pull one of the teenage kids out of school and send him to work, or be so screwed by welfare or social security or the UMW pension managers or the mine operators' disability insurance company that the meager payments that do come into some homes will be stopped.)

The truck mines play an ironic role in the local economy: half the men working in them, according to Holcomb, cannot work in the large mines because of physical disability. The small mines, in effect, not only get the leftover coal seams that aren't fat enough to interest Consol or U.S. Steel or the other big companies in the area, but they also get the men those firms have used up and discarded.

From Holcomb's point of view things are going pretty well in Pike County. In 1960 there were $18 million in deposits in Pikeville's three banks; that has risen to $65 million. There are 700 small mines in the county, many of them operated by former miners. "This is free enterprise at its finest," he said.

The next morning he took us on a trip through the Johns Creek area. As we passed new houses and large trailers he pointed to them as evidence of progress, which they in fact are. In the hollows behind, Fred and I could see the shacks and boxes in which people also live, and those Holcomb passed without a word. I suppose one must select from all the data presenting itself in this world, otherwise living gets awfully complex.

We drove up the hill to a small mine. Holcomb told us that the eight men working there produce 175 tons daily, all of which goes to the DuPont nylon plant in South Carolina.

A man in a shed just outside the mine mouth was

switching the heavy industrial batteries on a coal tractor. The miner was coated with coal dust and oil smears. He wore a plastic helmet with a light on it; around his waist was the light's battery pack, like a squashed holster. He moved very fast, whipping the chains off and on and winding the batteries out, pumping the pulley chains up and down. Another mine tractor crashed out of the entrance, its driver inclined at 45 degrees. The tractor is about 24 inches high and the mine roof is only 38 inches high, so the drivers have to tilt all the time or get their heads crushed. Inside, the men work on their knees. The tractor backed the buggy connected to it to the edge of a platform, dumped its load, then clanked back inside.

I went into the mine, lying on my side in the buggy towed by the tractor with the newly charged batteries.

Inside is utter blackness, broken only by the slicing beams of light from the helmets. The beams are neat and pretty, almost like a lucite tube poking here and there; the prettiness goes away when you realize the reason the beam is so brilliant is because of the coal and rock dust in the air, dust a worker is continually inhaling into his lungs. One sees no bodies, just occasional hands interrupting the moving lightbeams playing on the timbers and working face. Clattering noises and shouts are strangely disembodied and directionless.

Outside, I dust off and we head back toward town in Holcomb's truck.

"The temperature in there is 68 degrees all the time," he says. "You work in air-conditioned comfort all year 'round. Most of these men, after they've been in the mine for awhile, wouldn't work above ground." (I find myself thinking of Senator Murphy of California who in his campaign explained the need for bracero labor: they stoop over better than Anglos do.) The miners, as I said, make $14 a day.

"When you see what's been accomplished here in the last ten years it makes the doings of the AVs and the others seem completely insignificant. And we didn't have outside money." The pitted and gouged road is one-lane and we find ourselves creeping behind a heavily loaded coal truck heading toward one of the tipples up the road. "We think welfare is fine, but it should be a temporary measure, not a permanent one. And any organization that encourages people to get on welfare is a detriment to the community." The truck up front gets out of our way, Holcomb shifts back to two-wheel drive, we pick up speed. "These poverty program people, what they tried to do is latch on to some mountain customs and try to convince people they have come up with something new."

He believes business will help everybody; he believes the poverty program has been bad business. He is enormously sincere. Everyone is enormously sincere down here, or so it seems.

So we drove and looked at the new mines and tipples and Robert Holcomb told us how long each had been there and what its tonnage was and how many people each mine employed and how many mines fed into each tipple. One of his companies, he told us, produced 350,000 tons of coal last year and operated at a profit of 15.7 cents per ton.

Hospital death certificates cite things like pneumonia and heart disease. There is no way of knowing how many of those result from black lung and silicosis. The mine owners say very few; the miners and their families say a great many indeed. A lot of men with coated lungs don't die for a long time, but they may not be good for much else meanwhile. Their lungs won't absorb much oxygen, so they cannot move well or fast or long.

"This is a one-industry area," Holcomb had said, "and if you can't work at that industry you can't work at anything." Right. And most of the residents—men wrinkled

or contaminated, widows, children—do not work at anything. Over 50 percent of the families in Pike County have
incomes below $3,000 per year. Like land torn by the
strip-mining operations, those people simply stay back in
the hollers out of sight and slowly erode.

We talked with an old man who had worked in the
mines for 28 years. He told us how he had consumed his
life savings and two years' time getting his disabled social
security benefits.

"See, I got third-stage silicosis and I've got prostate and
gland trouble, stomach troubles, a ruptured disc. Now they
say that at the end of this month they're gonna take the
state aid medical card away. And that's all I've got; I've got
so much wrong with me I can't get no insurance. I've had
the card two years and now they say I draw too much
social security because of last year's increase in social
security benefits and they're gonna have to take my
medical card away from me after this month. I don't know
what in the hell I'm gonna do. Die, I reckon."

"Yeah, yeah," his wife said from the sink.

"It don't seem right," he said. "I worked like hell, I
made good money and I doublebacked. Because I worked a
lot and draw more social security than lots of people in the
mines where they don't make no money, I don't see where
it's right for them not to allow me no medical card."

He opened the refrigerator and showed us some of the
various chemicals he takes every day. In a neat stack on the
table were the month's medical receipts. He said something
about his youth, and I was suddenly stunned to realize he
was only 51.

"You know," he said, "sand's worse than black lung.
Silicosis. It hardens on the lung and there's no way to get it
off. In West Virginia I worked on one of those roof-bolting
machines. It's about eight, nine-foot high, sandstone top.

Burn the bits up drillin' holes in it. And I'd be there. Dust'd be that thick on your lips. But it's fine stuff in the air, you don't see the stuff that you get in your lungs. It's fine stuff. Then I didn't get no pay for it."

"You got a thousand dollars," his wife said.

"A thousand dollars for the first stage. They paid me first stage and I just didn't want to give up. I kept on workin', and now I got third stage. . . . I just hated to give up, but I wished I had of. One doctor said to me, 'If you keep on you might as well get your shotgun and shoot your brains out, you'd be better off.' I still kept on after he told me that. Then I got so I just couldn't hardly go on. My clothes wouldn't stay on me."

The woman brought coffee to the table. "He draws his disabled social security now," she says, "but if he was to draw for his black lung disease they would cut his social security way down, so he's better off just drawing his social security. There's guys around here they cut below what they was drawing for social security. I don't think that's right."

It is all very neat: the black lung, when a miner can force the company doctors to diagnose it honestly, is paid for by company insurance, but payments are set at a level such that a disabled miner loses most of his social security benefits if he takes the compensation; since the compensation pays less than social security, many miners don't put in their legitimate claims, and the net effect is a government subsidy of the insurance companies and mine owners.

Mary Walton, an Appalachian Volunteer, invited Fred and me to dinner at her place in Pikeville one night during our stay. It turned out Mary and I had been at Harvard at the same time and we talked about that place for a while, which was very strange there between those darkening hills. Three other people were at Mary's apartment: a girl named Barbara, in tight jeans and a white shirt with two buttons open and zippered boots, and two men, both of them connected with the local college. One was working with the Model Cities project, the other worked in the college president's office; one was astoundingly tall, the other was built like a wrestler; they all looked aggressively healthy. Barbara's husband worked for the Council of the Southern Mountains in Berea.

The fellow who looked like a wrestler told me at great length that what was going on in Pikeville wasn't a social or economic attack on the community structure, but rather an attack on the structure of ideas and only now was everyone learning that. I asked him what he meant. He said that the poverty workers had once seen their job as enlightening the masses about how messed up things were. "We were ugly Americans, that's all we were. That's why we weren't effective. But now we've learned that you don't change anything that way, you have to get inside the local community and understand it first and work there."

I thought that was indeed true, but I didn't see what it had to do with the structure of the community's ideas; it had to do only with the arrogance or naivete of the poverty workers, and that was awfully solipsistic. He hadn't said anything about his clients—just himself, just the way his ideas were challenged, not theirs.

The apartment was curiously out of that world. On the walls were posters and lithos and prints and pictures of healthy human bodies looking delicious. The record racks contained the Stones and *Tim Hardin No. 3* and a lot of Bach. Many of the recent books we'd all read and others one had and the others meant to, and Mary and I talked about them, but there was something relative, even in the pleasantness, as if it were an appositive in the bracketing nastiness out there.

When we got back to the car I took from my jacket pocket the heavy and uncomfortable shiny chromeplated .380 automatic pistol someone had once given me in San Antonio. I put it on the seat next to Fred's .357 revolver. They looked silly there; real guns always do. But people kept telling us how someone else was going to shoot us, or they recounted the story of how Hugh O'Connor, a Canadian film producer down in the next county the year before to make a movie, was shot in the heart by a man with no liking for outsiders and less for outsiders with cameras, and it did seem awfully easy to be an outsider here.

We went to see Edith Easterling, a lifelong Marrowbone Creek resident, working at that time for the Appalachian Volunteers as director of the Marrowbone Folk School. "The people in the mountains really lives hard," Edith said. "You can come into Pikeville and go to the Chamber of Commerce and they'll say, 'Well, there's really no poor people left there. People are faring good.' Then you can come out here and go to homes and you'd just be surprised how poor these people live, how hard that they live. Kids that's grown to 15 or 16 years old that's never had a mess of fresh milk or meats, things that kids really need. They live on canned cream until they get big enough to go to the table and eat beans and potatoes."

She told us about harassment and redbaiting of the AVs by Robert Holcomb, Harry Eastburn (the Big Sandy Community Action Program director, also funded by OEO, a bitter antagonist of any poverty program not under his political control), and Thomas Ratliff, the commonwealth's attorney (the equivalent of a county prosecutor).

Some of the AVs came from out of state, especially the higher paid office staff and technical specialists, but most of the 14 field workers were local people, like Edith. Since becoming involved with the poverty program Edith has received telephone threats and had some windows shot out. The sheriff refused to send a deputy to investigate. Occasionally she gets anonymous calls; some are threats, some call her "dirty communist." She shrugs those away: "I'm a Republican and who ever seen a communist Republican?"

The Appalachian Volunteers began in the early 1960s as a group of students from Berea College who busied themselves with needed community band-aid work: they made trips to the mountains to patch up dilapidated schoolhouses, they ran tutorial programs, they collected books for needy schools. The ultimate futility of such work soon became apparent and there was a drift in the AV staff toward projects that might affect the life style of some of the mountain communities. In 1966 the AVs decided to break away from their parent organization, the conservative Council of the Southern Mountains. The new, independent Appalachian Volunteers had no difficulty finding federal funding. During the summers of 1966 and 1967 the organization received large OEO grants to host hundreds of temporary volunteer workers, many of them VISTA and Peace Corps trainees. According to David Walls, who was acting director of the AVs when I talked with him, the organization's mission was to "create effective, economically self-sufficient poor people's organizations that would concern themselves with local issues, such as welfare rights, bridges and roads, water systems and strip mining."

It didn't work, of course it didn't work; the only reason it lasted as long as it did was because so much of the AV staff was composed of outsiders, people who had worked in San Francisco and Boston and New York and Washington, and it took a long time before the naivete cracked enough for the failure to show through.

The first consequence of creating an organization of the impoverished and unempowered is not the generation of any new source or residence of power, but rather the gathering in one place of a lot of poverty and powerlessness that previously were spread out. In an urban situation, the poor or a minority group may develop or exercise veto power: they can manage an economic boycott, they can refuse to work for certain firms and encourage others to join with them, they can physically block a store entrance. It is only when such efforts create a kind of negative monopoly (a strike line no one will cross or a boycott others will respect) that power is generated. When that negative monopoly cannot be created, there is no power—this is why workers can successfully strike for higher wages but the poor in cities cannot get the police to respect their civil liberties enough to stop beating them up; if everyone refuses to work at a factory, the owner must cooperate or close down, but there is nothing anyone can refuse a policeman that will remove the immediate incentive for illegal police behavior. The poor in the mountains cannot strike—they are unemployable anyway, or at least enough of them are to make specious that kind of action. Even if they were to get something going the UMW would not support them. The poor cannot start an economic boycott: they don't spend enough to hold back enough to threaten any aspect of the mountain coal economy. (There have been a few instances of industrial sabotage—I'll mention them later on—that have been dramatic, but pitifully ineffective.) One of the saddest things about the poor in the mountains is they have nothing to deny anyone. And they don't even have the wild hope some city poor entertain that something may turn up; in the mountains there is nothing to hope for.

Another problem with organizations of the very poor is they do not have much staying power: the individual participants are just too vulnerable. So long as the members can be scared or bought off easily, one cannot hope for such groups to develop solidarity. In Kentucky, where welfare, medical aid, disability pensions and union benefits all have a remarkable quality of coming and going with political whims, that is a real problem. Edith Easterling described the resulting condition: "These people are scared people, they are scared to death. I can talk to them and I can say, 'You shouldn't be scared, there's nothing to be scared about.' But they're still scared."

"What are they scared of," Fred asked her, "losing their jobs?"

"No. Some of 'em don't even have a job. Most of the people don't have jobs. They live on some kind of pension. They're scared of losing their pension. If it's not that, they're scared someone will take them to court for something. 'If I say something, they're going to take me to court and I don't have a lawyer's fee. I don't have a lawyer, so I'd rather not say nothing.' When you get the people to really start opening up and talking, that's when the country officials attack us every time with something."

For someone who brings troublesome publicity to the community, there are forms of retaliation far crueler than the mere cutting off of welfare or unemployment benefits. One poverty worker told of an event following a site visit by Robert Kennedy a few years ago: "When Kennedy was down for his hearings one of his advance men got in contact with a friend of ours who had a community organization going. They were very anxious to get some exposure, to get Kennedy involved in it. They took the advance men around to visit some families that were on welfare. He made statements about the terrible conditions the children there in two particular homes had to live under. He wasn't indicting the families, he was just talking about conditions in general. These were picked up by the local press and given quite a bit of notoriety—Kennedy Aide Makes the Scene, that sort of thing. After he left, about three days later, the welfare agency came and took away the children from both of those families and put them in homes. . . . This is the control that is over people's lives."

The group with the potential staying power in the mountains is the middle class, the small landowners. They have concrete things to lose while the poor (save in anomalous atrocities such as the one with the children mentioned above) have nothing to lose, they only have possible access to benefits that someone outside their group may or may not let them get. There is a big difference in the way one fights in the two situations. Something else: it is harder to scare the middle class off, for it has not been conditioned by all those years of humiliating control and dependency.

One Appalachian Volunteer, Joe Mulloy, a 24-year-old Kentuckian, realized this. He and his wife decided to join a fight being waged by a Pike County landowner, Jink Ray, and his neighbors, against a strip-mine operator who was about to remove the surface of Ray's land.

The focus of the fight was the legitimacy of the *broad-form* deed, a nineteenth century instrument with which landowners assigned mineral rights to mining companies, usually for small sums of money (50 cents per acre was common). When these deeds were originally signed no landowner had any thought of signing away all rights to his property—just the underground minerals and whatever few holes the mining company might have to make in the hillside to get at the seams. In the twentieth century the coal companies developed the idea of lifting off all the earth and rock above the coal, rather than digging for it, and since the broadform deed said the miner could use whatever means he saw fit to get the coal out, the Kentucky courts held that the miners' land rights had precedence over the surface owners'—even though that meant complete destruction of a man's land by a mining process the original signer of the deed could not have imagined. The strip miners are legally entitled, on the basis of a contract that might be 90 years old, to come to a man's home and completely bury it in rubble, leaving the owner nothing but the regular real estate tax bill with which he is stuck even though the "real estate" has since been dumped in the next creekbed. First come the bulldozers to do the initial clearing (a song I heard in West Virginia, to the tune of "Swing Low, Sweet Chariot," went: "Roll on, big D-9 dozer, comin' for to bury my home/ I'm getting madder as you're gettin' closer, comin' for to bury my home."), then they roll in the massive shovels, some of which are as large as 18.5 million pounds and can gobble 200 tons of earth and rock a minute and dump it all a city block away. Such a machine is operated by one man riding five stories above the ground.

On June 29, 1967, Jink Ray and some neighbors in Island Creek, a Pike County community, blocked with their bodies bulldozers that were about to start stripping Ray's land. With them were Joe and Karen Mulloy. The people themselves had organized the resistance; the Mulloys were simply helping.

With the strip-mining fight on the mountain, the AVs were for the first time involved in something significant. It was also dangerous: the members of the Island Creek group were challenging not only the basis of the local economy, but the federal government as well: the big mines' biggest customer is the Tennessee Valley Authority, and the Small Business Administration supports many of the smaller mine operators. The poverty program and other federal agencies were moving toward open conflict.

What happened was that the poverty program backed down and the local power structure moved in. Eleven days after Governor Edward Breathitt's August 1 suspension of the strip-mine company's Island Creek permit (the first and only such suspension), Pike County officials arrested the Mulloys for sedition (plotting or advocating the violent overthrow of the government). Arrested with them on the same charge were Alan and Margaret McSurely, field workers for the Southern Conference Educational Fund (SCEF), a Louisville-based civil rights organization. McSurely had been hired as training consultant by the AVs during the spring of 1967, but the real reason he had been hired was to restructure the cumbersome organization. One of the first things he did was get the AVs to allow local people on the board of directors; he was fired in a month and went to work for SCEF; they even arrested Carl Braden (SCEF's executive director) and his wife, Anne. Anne Braden had never been in Pike County in her life; the first time Carl Braden had been there was the day he went to Pikeville to post bail for McSurely on the sedition charge.

In Washington, the response to the arrests was immediate; Sargent Shriver's office announced that AV funds would be cut off; no funds previously granted were taken away, but no new money was appropriated after that.

The Pike County grand jury concluded that "a well-organized and well-financed effort is being made to promote and spread the communistic theory of violent and forceful overthrow of the government of Pike County." The grand jury said also that "communist organizers have attempted, without success thus far, to promote their beliefs among our school children by infiltrating our local schools with teachers who believe in the violent overthrow of the local government." Organizers were "planning to infiltrate local churches and labor unions in order to cause dissension and to promote their purposes." And, finally, "communist organizers are attempting to form community unions with the eventual purpose of organizing armed groups to be known as 'Red Guards' and through which the forceful overthrow of the local government would be accomplished."

The AVs came unglued. The Mulloys became pariahs within the organization. "We spent that whole summer and no AV came to see us at all in Pike County," Joe Mulloy said. "Once they came up to shit on us, but that was the only time. Then the thing of our getting arrested for sedition was what just really flipped everybody. . . . This was a real situation that you had to deal with, it wasn't something in your mind or some ideological thing. It was real. Another person was under arrest. I think that the feeling of a number of people on the staff was it was my fault that I had been arrested because I had been reckless in my organizing, that I had been on the mountain with the fellas and had risked as much as they were risking and I deserved what I got, and that I should be fired so the program would go on; that was now a detriment."

That fall, a special three-judge federal court ruled the Kentucky sedition law unconstitutional so all charges against the Mulloys, the Bradens and the McSurelys were wiped out. But the AVs were still nervous. "After the arrests were cleared away," Mulloy said, "things started to happen to me on the staff. I was given another assignment. I was told that I couldn't be a field man any more because I was a public figure identified with sedition and hence people would feel uneasy talking to me, and that I should do research. My truck was taken away and I was given an old car, and I was given a title of researcher rather than field man. It took away considerable voice that I had in the staff until then."

Karen Mulloy said she and Joe really had no choice. "If we had organized those people up there, with possible death as the end result for some of them—fortunately it was kept nonviolent—and if we weren't with them they wouldn't have spoken to us. We took as much risk as they did. We said to them, 'We're not going to organize something for you that we won't risk our necks for either.' An organizer can't do that."

"These people have gone through the whole union experience and that has sold them out," Joe said. "And a great number of people have gone through the poverty war experience and that hasn't answered anybody's problems, anybody's questions. Getting together on the strip-mining issue—if there was ever one issue that the poverty war got on that was good, that was it. It all fell through because when we started getting counterattacked by the operators the poverty war backed up because their funds were being jeopardized. The whole strip-mining issue as an organized effort has collapsed right now and the only thing that's going on is individual sabotage. There's a lot of mining equipment being blown up every month or so, about a million dollars at a time. These are individual or small group acts of retaliation, but the organized effort has ceased."

(Later, I talked with Rick Diehl, the AV research director, about the sabotage. He described two recent operations, both of them very sophisticated, involving groups of multiple charges set off simultaneously. The sheriff didn't even look for the dynamiters: he probably wouldn't have caught them and even if he had he wouldn't have gotten a jury to convict. "And that kind of stuff goes on to some degree all the time," Diehl said. "There's a growing feeling that destroying property is going to shut down the system in Appalachia. The people don't benefit from the coal companies at all, 'cause even the deep mines don't have enough employees. The average number of employees in a deep mine is 16 people. So, you can see, there is nothing to lose. It's that same desperation kind of thing that grips people in Detroit and Watts.")

Even though the sedition charges were dropped, the Mulloys and McSurelys weren't to escape punishment for their organizing outrages.

One Friday the 13th Al McSurely came home late from a two- or three-day trip out of town, talked with his wife a little while, then went to bed. Margaret went to bed a short time later. "I wasn't asleep at all," she said, "but he was so tired he went right to sleep. I heard this car speed up. Well, I had got into the habit of listening to cars at night, just because we always expected something like this to happen. And sure enough, it did. There was this blast. The car took off and there was this huge blast, and glass and dirt and grit were in my mouth and eyes and hair, and the baby was screaming. So I put on my bathrobe and ran across the street with the baby."

"The state trooper was pretty good," Alan said. "He gave me a lecture: 'The next time this happens call the city police first so they can seal off the holler. They can get here much faster than I can.' I said, 'I'll try and remember that.' "

Joe Mulloy was the only AV with a Kentucky draft board; he was also the only AV to lose his occupational deferment and have his 2-A changed to 1-A. Mulloy asked the board (in Louisville, the same as Muhammed Ali's) for a rehearing on the grounds of conscientious objection, and he presented as part of his evidence a letter from Thomas Merton saying he was Mulloy's spiritual adviser (the two used to meet for talks in Merton's cabin in the woods) and could testify to the truthfulness of Mulloy's

C.O. claim. The board refused to reopen the case because, they said, there was no new evidence of any relevance or value. In April 1968 Mulloy was sentenced to five years in prison and a $10,000 fine for refusing induction.

He was fired immediately by the Appalachian Volunteers. Some wanted him out because they honestly thought his draft case would be a major obstacle to his effectiveness with the oddly patriotic mountain people. (In the mountains you can be against the war, many people are, but if your country calls you, you go. It would be unpatriotic not to go. The government and the country are two quite independent entities. The government might screw up the poverty program, run that bad war, work in conjunction with the mine owners and politicians, but it isn't the government that is calling you—it is the country. Only a weirdo would refuse that call. But once you're in you are working for the government, and then it is all right to desert.) Others on the AV staff objected to Mulloy's getting involved in issues that riled up the authorities. The staff vote to get rid of him was 20 to 19.

What the AVs failed to admit was that the changing of Mulloy's draft status was an attack on them as well: the only reason for the change was the strip-mine fight. The draft board had joined the OEO, the TVA, the mine owners, the political structure of the state and the UMW in opposition to effective organization of the poor in the mountains.

I asked Joe how he felt about it all now. "I don't know if I can really talk about this objectively," he said. "I feel in my guts as a Kentuckian a great deal of resentment against a lot of these people. And some of them are my friends that have come in and stirred things up and then have left. The going is really tough right now. I'm still here, all the people that have to make a living out in those counties are still there with their black lung. I don't think anything was accomplished. It's one of those things that's going to go down in history as a cruel joke: the poverty war in the mountains."

The two bad guys of the story, I suppose, should be Robert Holcomb, spokesman for the mine owners in the county, and commonwealth's attorney Thomas Ratliff, the man who handled the prosecution in the sedition and who was (coincidentally, he insists) Republican candidate for lieutenant governor at the time; Ratliff got rich in the mine business, but is now into a lot of other things. Like most bad guy labels, I suspect these are too easy. I'll come back to that.

I rather liked Ratliff even though there were things I knew about him I didn't like at all. It is quite possible he really does believe, as he said he does, that the McSurelys and the Bradens are communist provocateurs; there are people in America who believe such menaces exist, though not very many of them are as intelligent as Ratliff.

He claims the defendants in the sedition case had "a new angle on revolution—to do it locally and then bring all the local revolutions together and then you got a big revolution. Now whether it would have succeeded or not I don't know. I think it possibly could have, had they been able to continue to get money from the Jolly Green Giant, as they call Uncle Sam. I certainly think with enough money, and knowing the history of this area, it was not impossible."

What seems to have bothered him most was not the politics involved but the bad sportsmanship: "The thing that rankled me in this case, and it still does, this is really what disturbed me more about this thing than anything else, was the fact that . . . they were able to use federal money . . . to promote this thing. Frankly, I would be almost as opposed to either the Republican party or the Democratic party being financed by the federal money to prevail, much less a group who were avowed communists, made no bones about it that I could tell, whose objective was revolution, the forceful and violent overthrow of the local government and hopefully to overthrow the federal government, and it was being financed by federal tax money!"

Once Ratliff got off his communist menace line, I found myself agreeing with him as much as I had with some of the remarks Joe Mulloy had made. Ratliff spoke eloquently on the need for a negative income tax, for massive increases on the taxes on the mine operators, things like that. (Whether he meant the things he said is impossible to tell; one never knows with politicians, or anyone else for that matter.)

"It's the reaction to this sort of situation that really bothers me," he said, "because—there is no question about it—there is some containment of free speech, free expression, when you get a situation like this. People become overexcited and overdisturbed. And the laws of physics play in these things: for every action there's a reaction, and the reaction, unfortunately, is often too much in this kind of situation. You begin seeing a communist behind every tree. That's bad. Because there isn't a communist behind every tree, or anything like that.

"But I think they've accomplished one thing, not what they thought they would. . . . That's the tragic part of it, I don't think they've uplifted anybody. I think they have left a lot of people disappointed, frustrated. . . . But I think they have scared the so-called affluent society into doing something about it. Maybe. I think there are people more conscious of it because of that."

It is so easy to write off Holcomb or Ratliff as evil men,

grasping and groping for whatever they can get and destroying whatever gets in the way; for a poverty worker it is probably necessary to think such thoughts, that may be the mental bracing one needs to deal as an opponent.

But I think it is wrong.

Holcomb is an ex-miner who made it; uneducated and not particularly smart, he somehow grooved on the leavings in that weird economy and got rich. He thinks what he did is something anyone ought to be able to do: it is the American dream, after all. His failure is mainly one of vision, a social myopia hardly rare in this country. From Holcomb's point of view, those people stirring up the poor probably are communist agitators—why else would anyone interfere with the "free enterprise system at its best"? If you tried to tell him that a system that leads to great big rich houses on one side of town and squalid leaky shacks on the other might not be the best thing in this world he'd think you were crazy or a communist (both, actually) too. And Thomas Ratliff is hardly the simple Machiavelli the usual scenario would demand.

Picking out individuals and saying the evil rests with them is like patching schoolhouses and expecting the cycle of poverty to be broken. Even when you're right you're irrelevant. What is evil in the mountains is the complex of systems, a complex that has no use or place or tolerance for the old, the wrecked, the incompetent, the extra, and consigns them to the same gullies and hollers and ditches as the useless cars and empty Maxwell House coffee tins and Royal Crown Cola cans, with the same lack of hate or love.

The enemies of the poverty program, malicious or natural, individual or collective, turn out to be far more successful than they could have hoped or expected. One reason for that success is the cooperation of the victims:

groups like the AVs become, as one of their long-time members said, "top-heavy and bureaucratic, a bit central office bound. We are . . . worried about maintaining the AV structure, and responding to pressures from foundations and OEO, rather than from community people." The federal government, presumably the opponent of poverty here, plays both sides of the fence: it supports activities like the AVs (so long as they are undisturbing), but it also supports the local Community Action Program, which is middle-class dominated and politically controlled; it created a generation of hustlers among the poor who find out that only by lying and finagling can they get the welfare and social security benefits they legitimately deserve; it strengthens the local courthouse power structures by putting federal job programs in control of the county machines and by putting the Small Business Administration at its disposal; it commissions studies to document the ill effects of strip mining and simultaneously acts, through TVA, as the largest consumer of the product.

The mood is much like the McCarthy days of the early 1950s: actual legal sanctions are applied to very few people, but so many others are smeared that other people are afraid of contagion, of contamination, even though they know there is nothing to catch. They avoid issues that might threaten some agency or person of power, they stop making trouble, stop looking for trouble, they keep busy, or they stay home—and no one ever really says, when faced by the complex, "I'm scared."

Everyone has something to do: busy, busy, busy. I remember a visit to the AV office in Prestonsburg; they had there what must have been one of the largest Xerox machines in the state of Kentucky; it was used for copying newspaper articles; someone on the staff ran it. There was an AV magazine assembled by a staff member who, if some of the foundations grants had come through, would have gotten a full-time assistant. The mining went on; the acting director of the AVs, Dave Walls, went about hustling private foundations grants and being sociable and vague and disarming to visitors, and not much of anything really happened.

I visited eastern Kentucky again a short time ago. There were some changes. The weather was softer and some leaves were on the trees, so you couldn't see the shacks back in the hollers unless you drove up close; you couldn't see the hillside cemeteries and junkyards at all.

I found out that Governor Louis Nunn had blocked any new AV funds and most of the other money had gone, so there were ugly battles over the leavings, mixed with uglier battles over old political differences within the organization itself.

Edith Easterling was fired; she now has a Ford grant to travel about the country and look at organizing projects. Rick Diehl has gone somewhere else. Mary Walton is now a staff reporter for the Charleston (W. Va.) *Gazette*. The Prestonsburg AV office is still open—with a small group of lawyers working on welfare rights problems; that is the only AV activity still alive and no one knows how much longer there will be any money for that.

I ran into Dave Walls in a movie house in Charleston. The show was *Wild River* with Montgomery Clift and Lee Remick, and it was about how good TVA is and what a swell guy Montgomery Clift is and how homey and true mountain girl Lee Remick is. Anyway, I saw Dave there and we talked a moment during intermission. He still draws a subsistence salary from the AVs, still lives in Berea, over in the Bluegrass country far and nicely away from it all. He is going to school at the University of Kentucky in Lexington, doing graduate work in something. He looked just the same, no more or less mild. Someone asked him, "What's going on in the mountains now? What happened to everything?" He shrugged and smiled, "I don't know," he said, "I haven't gone to the mountains in a long time."

Well, for the other people, the ones who were there before, things are pretty much the same. That woman and her nine children still live in that shack in Poorbottom. The man who worked the mines for 28 years is still kept marginally alive by the chemical array in his refrigerator he still somehow manages to afford.

Jink Ray, the man who faced down the bulldozers, I met on that recent trip. When we drove up he had just put out some bad honey and the bees were a thick swarm in the front of the house. We went into a sitting room-bedroom where his wife sat before an open coal fire and each wall had one or two Christs upon it. We talked about the strip-mine fight. On one wall was a photo of him with Governor Breathitt the day the governor came up to stop the strippers. We went outside and talked some more, standing by the overripe browning corn standing next to a patch of corn just about ripe, the hills thickly coated and overlapping to form a lush box canyon behind him. He pointed to the hillside the other side of the road and told us they'd been augering up there. "You can't see it from down here this time of year, but it's bad up there." The seepage killed the small streams down below: nothing lives in those streams anymore. "We used to get bait in them streams, nothing now, and fish used to grow there before they went to the river. Not now." Suddenly his face hardened, "Why you fellas asking me these questions?" We told him again that we were writing about what had happened in Pike County. "No," he said, "that ain't what you are. I believe you fellas are here because you want to get stripping going again, you want to know if I'll back off this time." He talked from a place far behind the cold blue eyes that were just so awful. We protested, saying we really were writers, but it didn't work—it's like denying you're an undercover agent or homosexual, there's no way in the world to do it once the assumption gets made, however wrong. He talked in postured and rhetorical bursts awhile and it seemed a long time until we could leave without seeming to have been run off. Leaving him standing there looking at the yellow Hertz car backing out his driveway, his face still cold and hard, polite to the end, but. . . . But what? Not hating, but knowing: he knows about strangers now, he knows they are there to take something away, to betray, to hustle, he knows even the friendly strangers will eventually go back wherever strangers go when they are through doing whatever they have come down to do, and he will be just where he is, trying with whatever meager resources he's got to hold on to the small parcel of land he scuffled so hard to be able to own. He'll not trust anyone again, and for me that was perhaps the most painful symptom of the failure and defeat of the poverty program in the mountains.

The others: Joe Mulloy, after about two years in the courts, finally won the draft appeal he should never have had to make in the first place; Al and Margaret McSurely were sentenced to prison terms for contempt of Congress after they refused to turn over their personal papers to a Senate committee investigating subversion in the rural South. Tom Ratliff is still commonwealth's attorney, there in the county of Pike, in the state of Kentucky. And Robert Holcomb still has his mines, his collieries, his offices, and his fine and unshaken belief in the American Way.

June 1971

On the Case
in Resurrection City

CHARLAYNE HUNTER

Resurrection City—where the poor had hoped to become visible and effective—is dead. And despite the contention of many people, both black and white, that it should never have been born, R.C. was, as its City Fathers had been quick to point out, a moment in history that may yet have a telling effect on the future of this country. For although Resurrection City was never really a city, per se, it functioned as a city, with all the elements of conflict that arise when public issues and private troubles come together.

The public issues were clear and could be articulated—at least in a general way—by most of the people who lived there. Handbills had helped residents formulate their statement of purpose. "What will the Poor People's Campaign do in Washington?" read one handbill. "We will build powerful nonviolent demonstrations on the issues of jobs, income, welfare, health, housing, human rights. These massive demonstrations will be aimed at government centers of power and they will be expanded if necessary. We must make the government face up to poverty and racism." If such a statement was not specific enough, residents—who in all probability found it difficult to always know just what the leaders had in mind (as did the leaders themselves)— would simply fend off the question with a statement like, "*We* know what the demands are." If pressed further, they would glare accusingly at the questioner, as if to further confirm his ignorance. (This technique of bluffing one's way into the offensive was initiated by the leader of the Poor People's Campaign, the Rev. Ralph Abernathy. The press was relentless in its efforts to get Mr. Abernathy to give out more specifics about his demands, but this was impossible for a long while simply because none had been formulated.)

The private troubles of those who came to live in R.C. were less clear, at least in the beginning. And as these troubles emerged—sometimes in the form of fights, rapes, thefts, and harassment—they became far more prominent than the cause or the individuals who came to fight for it. The outside world concerned itself with the disorganization and lack of leadership in the camp. And while this was certainly a valid concern, critics seemed to be missing one essential point—that the life styles of the poor vary, from individual to individual and from region to region. Long before coming to Resurrection City, leaders and followers had been conditioned by their backgrounds and the life styles they had established. That is why, for example, the first City Manager of R.C., Jesse Jackson—a 26-year-old Chicagoan and an official of the Southern Christian Leadership Conference (S.C.L.C.)—had more success with the Northern urban hustler than did Hosea Williams, the second City Manager, who came out of the South and had much more success with diffident rural blacks.

Most of the conflicts at the camp were caused by the ghetto youths whose lives in the asphalt jungles of the North led them to view Resurrection City as a camp-outing and an alfresco frolic. Surrounded by trees, grass, and open air, the Northern youths were among alien things, which (before the rain and mud) were hostile to them. The innocence of their Southern counterparts—for whom the trees, grass, open air, and mud are a way of life—was a challenge to the Northerners. With such easy, church-oriented prey, the hip cat from the North immediately went into his thing—taking advantage of the uninitiated. Southerners had the history of the movement behind them. They had produced the sit-ins, the Freedom Rides, the Bus Boycotts—the 1960's Direct Action Task Force. And yet much of the Southern mystique got beaten by the hard, hostile life style of the urban ghetto-dweller.

No one is quite sure how many people moved into Resurrection City, although there was an attempt to register people as they came in. The registration count was 6312, but the community was nothing if not mobile and there was no way to count the outflow.

The people came to the District from all sections of the country. They came in bus caravans and on trains. Some came from the South in the Mule Train (which was put into a regular train in Atlanta because the horses were giving out), some came from the nearby North in cars or on foot. They came representing the church. They came representing the community. They came representing street gangs—those that would fight and those that wouldn't. And many came representing themselves. Most came as followers. But, of necessity, a few emerged as leaders. Many came to participate in the campaign for as long as S.C.L.C. wanted them there, and then they planned to go home. Others came thinking of the North as a land of opportunity. And *they* came to stay forever.

Today, the site where Resurrection City stood is cleared. After the sun baked the mud dry, patches of growing grass were placed there, and although the land is not quite so green as it was before, it is just as it was when the architects began designing Resurrection City on paper back in April. Perhaps if they had it to do over, they would change a few things, because, by now, they would have learned about the differences in poverty—that poor people do not automatically respond positively to one another.

The design, on paper, had been impressive. Three architects (none of them Negroes), with the help of students of the Howard University School of Architecture (all of them Negroes), produced plans that called for modest A-frame structures, which could be built small enough for two and large enough for six or eight and which would house 3000 people for two to four months. The prefabricated units—25 percent of them A-frames and 75 percent of them dormitories—were to be assembled in Virginia by local white volunteers, then brought to Washington in trucks that would be unloaded next to the building sites, starting west and building eastward.

By the time the first stake for an A-frame was driven in by Mr. Abernathy, around a thousand people had already come into Washington and had been housed in coliseums and churches.

During the first week, morale and energy and activity levels were high. But one of the first indications that the paper plans might not succeed came when the New York delegation insisted upon setting up shop in the most easternward section of the site. New Yorkers, independent, fast-paced, and accustomed to protests (like rent strikes) that require organization, were going to do things their own way. Though this meant that they had to carry their own wood all the way from the front of the site to the back, they set up their structures with record-breaking speed. Where it sometimes took three men working together an hour to put up an A-frame, in the New York contingent three men produced an A-frame in 15 minutes. There was, among *everyone,* a feeling of distrust for larger communities: Provincialism had reared its head.

After a week and a half of more or less organized endeavor, there followed a long stretch of bad weather. It rained every day, and rivers of thick, brown mud stood in doorways and flowed along the walkways from one end of the camp to the other. But although the mud and rain sapped some of the energy of some of the assemblers, it seemed to inspire creativity in others—the majority, in fact, since they were eager to get their houses built so that they could move in. More people came to R.C. than left. And although many had been evacuated to churches and schools—often long distances away—the Mexican-Americans and the Indians were the only contingents that chose to stay on high ground.

When the rains did not let up, the last vestiges of formal organization at R.C. slid unceremoniously into the mud. But those who had left returned, and others joined them, and all waded through. Wood that had been lost turned up as porches for the A-frame houses—luxuries not called for in the paper plans. "It was interesting to see this mass-produced, prefab stuff developing into color and rambunctiousness," one of the planners said.

By the time most of the A-frames had been filled, what existed on the site of the planned city was a camp rather than a community, with some areas so compounded with picket fences or solid fences that no outsider could get in. Walking or wading through the camp, one saw not only simple, unadorned A-frames, but split-levels and duplexes. Some were unpainted; others were painted simply (usually with yellows and burgundy) ; and still others were both mildly and wildly, reverently and irreverently, decorated with slogans. One house bore on its side a verse from the Bible: "And they said one to another, behold, this dreamer cometh. Come now therefore, and let us slay him, and cast him into some pit, and we will say, some evil beast hath devoured him: and we shall see what will become of his dreams. Genesis 37. Martin Luther King, Jr., 1929-1968." Others had such slogans as "Black Power on Time," "Soul Power," "United People Power, Toledo, Ohio," "Soul City, U.S.A.," and "The Dirty Dozen," on a building I figured was a dormitory. And, of course, the inevitable "Flower Power." "I Have a Dream" stickers appeared in most places, as well as pictures of Martin Luther King—usually enshrined beside the canvas-and-wood cots inside the houses.

Just as the slogans varied widely, so did the inside appearance of the houses. While many looked like the wreck of the Hesperus, in others, by 9 A.M. when the camp was opened to visitors, beds were made, clothes were hung, floors were swept, and—in several houses—plank coffee-tables were adorned with greenery in tin-can vases.

The Coretta King Day Care Center was perhaps the most successful unit in the camp. A local church group contributed most of the materials, including books like *Alice in Wonderland*, *What Are You Looking At?*, *The Enormous Egg*, and Bennett Cerf's *Pop-Up Lyrics*. There were even toy cars and trucks, water colors, and jigsaw puzzles. And a hundred pairs of muddy boots. The children played games and sang songs such as "If You're Happy and You Know It, Clap Your Hands" and, of course, "We Shall Overcome." And they went on field trips—to the Smithsonian, the National Historical Wax Museum, and Georgetown University. Enrollment was about 75.

Altogether, Resurrection City never contained more than the average American city—the bare-bone necessities. Still, many people received more medical attention than ever before in their lives. A young mother left Marks, Miss., with a baby whose chances of survival, she had been told, were very slim. He was dying of malnutrition. After three weeks of medical care—vitamins, milk, food—he began gaining weight and life. For others, teeth were saved. Upper-respiratory infections—at one point a source of alarm to those outside the camp—were treated and curbed. And when one of the residents died while on a demonstration in the food line at the Agriculture Department, there was little doubt that it was not Resurrection City that killed him, but the lack of adequate medical attention back home. Most of the residents were also eating better. The menus were often a hodge-podge affair—sometimes consisting of beef stew, turnip greens, apple sauce, and an orange—but the food was nutritious. And you did not need food stamps to get it.

Residents of Resurrection City found it difficult to understand the outside world's reaction via the press to conditions within the camp. The stink from the toilets that filled one's nostrils whenever a breeze stirred was, as one observer put it, "the smell of poverty." Residents put it another way. "I appreciate the mud," a woman from Detroit said. "It might help get some of this disease out."

The mud of Resurrection City was seen by many as unifying, if not cleansing. Andy Young, an S.C.L.C. executive, trying to dispel rumors of disorganization in the camp, said one day: "We are a movement, not an organization. And we move when the spirit says move. Anything outside is God's business. We are incorporated by the Lord and baptized by all this rain."

While the camp was virtually leaderless from a formal, organizational standpoint (Mr. Abernathy was always off traveling with a large entourage of S.C.L.C. officials), it did not lack individual movers and doers. One day, a discussion of the mud revealed such a person. Standing attentively at a press conference on a sunny day, with an umbrella over her head, Mrs. Lila Mae Brooks of Sunflower County, Miss., said, to no one in particular, "We used to mud and us who have commodes are used to no sewers." A tall, thin, spirited woman, Mrs. Brooks talks with little or no prompting. Observing that I was interested, she went on: "We used to being sick, too. And we used to death. All my children [she has eight] born sickly. But in Sunflower County, sick folks sent from the hospital and told to come back in two months. They set up 27 rent houses—rent for $25—and they put you out when you don't pay. People got the health department over 'bout the sewers, but Mayor said they couldn't put in sewers until 1972." She is 47, and for years has worked in private homes, cotton fields, and churches. In 1964 she was fired from a job for helping Negroes register to vote. For a while, she was on the S.C.L.C. staff, teaching citizenship. When she had a sunstroke, and later a heart attack, she had to go on welfare. (She is also divorced.) For three years, she got $40-a-month child support, and finally $73. She left her children with her mother, who is 80, and sister to come to the campaign.

"People in Sunflower asked my friends was I sick 'cause they hadn't seen me. Then they saw me on TV in Washington and said I'd better head back before the first or they'd cut off my welfare check. You go out the state overnight and they cut off your welfare check. But that's OK. I had to come. When S.C.L.C. chose me from Eastland's County, he met his match. I've seen so much. I've seen 'em selling food stamps and they tell you if you don't buy, they cut off your welfare check. And that stuff they sell there don't count—milk, tobacco, and washing powder. Well, how you gonna keep clean? All the welfare people know is what *they* need. I ain't raising no more white babies for them. Ain't goin' that road no more. I drug my own children through the cotton fields, now they talkin' 'bout not lettin' us go to Congress. Well, I'll stand on Eastland's toes. People from 12 months to 12 months without work. People with no money. Where the hell the money at? I say to myself, I'll go to Washington and find out. Talking about using it to build clinics. Then they make people pay so much at the clinics they get turned away. What the people gettin' ain't enough to say grace over. I done wrote to Washington so much they don't have to ask my name."

I asked Mrs. Brooks how long she planned to say here. "I don't know, honey," she said as she put her sunglasses on. "They just might have to 'posit my body in Washington."

There were other women organizing welfare groups and working in the lunch halls, and still others, like Miss Muriel Johnson, a social worker on loan to S.C.L.C. from other organizations. This was her first movement and she was in charge of holding "sensitivity" sessions. When I asked her what a sensitivity session was, she said, "Well, you just can't take a bunch of people out and march them down Independence Avenue. All they know is that they're hungry and want something done about it. We got 150 to 200 people out a day into nonviolent demonstrations. We got to teach them to protect themselves and prepare for whatever. We have to explain situations to people. And we have to talk with them, not down to them. If they get something out of this training, they'll go home and do something."

Joining Mrs. Brooks and Miss Johnson were many other young men and women, among them college students who, like the students of the old movement (the early 1960s), believed that it was better for black boys and girls to give themselves immediately and fully to a worthwhile cause than to finish college. Many of them wore their hair natural and some wore buttons that said, "Doing it black." Young men like Leon and J.T., both S.C.L.C. organizers in the South, held no place in the movement hierarchy, but were, as the residents were fond of saying of anybody plugged in to what was going on, "on the case."

Leon and J.T. led demonstrations and boosted morale by taking part in the day-to-day problems and activities of Resurrection City. The difference between them and many of the other S.C.L.C. officials was that when R.C. residents were tired and smelly from marching eight miles to a demonstration and back, so were Leon and J.T. When residents went to bed wearing all their clothes and wrapped in blankets saturated with dampness, so did Leon and J.T. And if Leon and J.T. could still sing freedom songs the next day, then so could they. There were not, however, enough Leons and J.T.s. Many weeks had been spent building the Abernathy compound—a large frame structure surrounded by A-frames for his aides. But despite a ceremonial gesture of walking in with a suitcase and announcing that he was moving in, Mr. Abernathy never lived in R.C. Nor did his lieutenants.

One of the most effective communicators around Resurrection City was a man of a different breed from that of Leon or J.T.: Lance Watson, better (and perhaps solely) known as Sweet Willie Wine. Sweet Willie, 29, is the leader of the Memphis Invaders, the group accused of starting the riots in Memphis after the assassination of Martin Luther King. (Sweet Willie denies this.) He spent most of his time walking around the camp, wrapped in a colorful serapi, combing his heavy Afro. He condemns the Vietnam war as immoral, and of his own time in the army paratroops says, "In service I took the great white father's word. I thought it was all right to be half a man. Now it is time to question. We are questioning everything now."

When the campaign was over, most of the Invaders went home. Sweet Willie, however, is still walking the streets of Washington, occasionally plugging in to local militants, but more often holding down some corner in the black ghetto.

The Invaders bridged the gap between the diffident Southern blacks and the hustling ghetto youth from the North. Memphis, after all, is a kind of half-way place, with elements both of the Southern rural and the urban ghetto scenes. And it is perhaps because of this that they made it through to the end. The Blackstone Rangers, from Chicago, did not. Early on, they were sent home for causing trouble. Acting on the theory that if the tough guys were used as peace officers, they would be too busy keeping others out of trouble to get in trouble themselves, S.C.L.C. officials began using the Blackstone Rangers as marshals. It didn't work.

Yet most of the gangs there saw themselves more as protectors of the other black people in the camp than as participants in the campaign. The leader of St. Louis's Zulu 1200's, Clarence Guthrie, said that the Zulus did not pretend to be nonviolent, but "since this campaign concerns a lot of brothers and sisters who are working their thing, we'll use our resources to protect them."

With so many disparate elements in the camp, it only took a slight incident to cause a large group to assemble, with a great deal of fight potential. Most of the Southerners had come with an S.C.L.C. orientation, and as a result they were still singing "We Shall Overcome," including the verse "Black and white together." But few people from above the Mason-Dixon line were singing "We Shall Overcome," let alone "Black and white together." They usually ignored the whites inside the camp, who for the most part were either kids who would do all the dirty work or hippies off somewhere by themselves with their flowers. Still, any altercation outside the camp usually involved some white person. Such was the case when a fight broke out just outside the grounds. Police—mostly whites—appeared in large numbers. The Tent City Rangers, a group of older men formed as security officers, broke up the fight, but some of the boys whose adrenaline had risen headed for a white man wearing bermuda shorts and taking pictures. With dispatch, they relieved him of his camera and disappeared. The man wanted his camera back, he said, because it was expensive. But he added, "I think I understand. I come down here in my bermuda shorts taking pictures. And I guess I understand how this would make them angry."

Laurice Barksdale, a 24-year-old veteran from Atlanta, was angry, too. But he vented his frustrations in another way. From early in the morning to late in the afternoon, the sweet smell of baking bread joined the other scents in the air. In a small A-frame decorated with the motto "Unhung-up Bread," Barksdale spent every day baking bread for residents and visitors as well. The supplies had come from a white New Yorker who travels from community to community teaching people how to make bread. At R.C. he discovered Barksdale, who had learned to cook in his high school home-economics class, and set him up in business. After four years in the Marines, Barksdale had come home to Atlanta and had not been able to find a job. His mother, who worked for S.C.L.C., suggested that he go along on the Poor People's Campaign to see if he could help out. Barksdale says he's not really interested in making money. "I got a cause," he says. "And a lot of brothers and sisters around me."

The one S.C.L.C. higher-up always on the case was Hosea Williams, who early in the campaign became the City Manager. One of Hosea's major assets was the gift of rap.

One Sunday morning he was stopped by three well-dressed white men, one of whom said he was running for Congress from Florida and had come to R.C. because he felt he and his people ought to know about it. Soon after the conversation began, the man asked Hosea about his background, and if he was a Communist. Hosea was not offended by the question, but moved into it slowly. He denied being a Communist.

"What is Resurrection City all about?" Hosea asked rhetorically. "This is what you have to know. We are asking for jobs. Not welfare. Check the cat on the welfare rolls and you'll find his mother and daddy were on welfare.

"What we've got to have is a redefinition of work. As Lillian Smith indicated in her book, I think *Killers of the Dream,* what we have is a conflicting ideology in our value system. The reason I loved Dr. King was that he made $600,000 in one year and died a pauper. We have got to let scientists go to work and create jobs. I know it can be done. I was working as a research chemist for 14 years trying to rid this country of insects. I was born in Attapulgus, Ga. My father was a field hand and my mother worked in the white folks' house. I raised myself while she raised the white folks' children. And we got to get some help for the old. And we got to do something about this educational system. That's what produced the hippies. White colleges. I got more respect for the hippies than I have for the hypocrites.

"R.C. is just a place we have to sleep and get some food to fight a war—a nonviolent war. We are here for an economic bill of rights. Congress's job is to solve the problems. We are political analysts and psychiatrists and Congress is the patient."

On that Sunday morning there was a sense of movement and activity throughout the camp. This was true on any given day. Near the entrance to the camp, young boys played checkers and whist, and some were getting haircuts. Over the P.A. system in City Hall, someone was calling for attention. "Will Cornbread please report to City Hall immediately? Attention. Will Cornbread please report to City Hall immediately?" Like Leon and J.T. most people didn't know any other name for Cornbread but Cornbread. But Cornbread was a household word because he was on the case.

Also on that morning, a tall, thin, white man looking like the church pictures of Jesus took up a position behind a table near the checkers game and began making predictions—that there would be a big snow in August; that there would be a Republican President in 1972; that people of America would one day eat one another.

"Are you open to question?" someone called out. He did not respond.

The thin man continued, saying that he had prophesied the burning in Washington. He was interrupted again, by another voice from what had become a building crowd. "Tell me what the number gon' be so I can be a rich man tomorrow." An elderly Negro man with a pair of crutches next to his chair called out, to no one in particular, "Hey, where are my cigars?"

I asked the crippled man where he came from. Coy, Ala. How long had he been at R.C.? "Since they drove the first nail," he answered. "What have you been doing?" "Well, I can't do much. I've got arthritis. I usually get up about 4 A.M. and just sit here. But I tried to organize a men's Bible class like at my church back home. Not too much success, though. I had a lovely time yesterday. Seven of us went out to a church and we had services. Then we had a wonderful dinner there—fried chicken, candied potatoes, and wrinkle steaks. You know what those are, don't you?" He smiled. "If I can hop a ride, I want to go back."

Sitting behind him were two young men. One was saying, "I got to fly home to court tomorrow. Charge of marihuana. Ain't had none." The young man was from New York. It was not the kind of thing one was likely to hear from his Southern counterpart. Narcotics is the traditional way out for many of the frustrated young in the asphalt jungles of the North. Somehow, this syndrome never hit the South. A young Southern black, eager to escape the lot of his father, has one way out—the army. And many of them, once they enlist, choose to stay.

Soon another announcement came over the P.A. system asking all residents who planned to take part in the day's demonstrations to report to the front gate.

On Sundays, Resurrection City—with all its diversity—was opened up to even more diversity. Sunday was tourist day and visitors began arriving sometime after breakfast. One particular Sunday, as the residents drifted out of the front gate to a demonstration, among the tourists coming in were many well-dressed Negroes from the District on their way home from church or elsewhere (as remote as they seemed to be from things, it didn't seem likely that they would have dressed up to come to R.C.). Some whites came, too. Mainly the tourists drove by in cars, slowing down long enough to snap a picture and continue on. To the Negro visitors (who almost never wore boots to protect their shoes from the mud), most residents (who did wear boots and slept in them at night to keep warm) were cordial, sometimes condescending (something of a unique turnabout in the scheme of things) — "Yes, *do* come in and have a look around. We're right proud of what we have here." Later, at a Lou Rawls concert, which was inadvertently set up before the demonstration, but which Hosea decided to let go on, Hosea addressed the crowd and concluded with a few well-chosen words for the Negro tourists: "The police want to use those billy clubs. But they ain't gonna bother you today. Today is Uncle Tom Day, and they don't whip up on Uncle Tom heads."

Demonstrations were the one constant in R.C. Each demonstration I attended was different from another, not so much because the body of demonstrators changed as because of their usual tendency to "do what the spirit say do."

Although R.C. residents had been there before—to present demands for changes in the welfare system—my first demonstration was at the Department of Health, Education, and Welfare. The 200 demonstrators marched into the auditorium of the building and sent word that they wanted to see "Brother Cohen"—Wilbur J. Cohen, Secretary of Health, Education, and Welfare. An otherwise impressive delegation—including Assistant Secretary Ralph K. Huitt and Harold Howe II of H.E.W.'s Office of Education— was sent in, but was given short shrift. Led by Hosea, the demonstrators began to chant "We want Cohen," and Hosea turned from the second-string officials and told the crowd: "You might as well get comfortable," and before he had finished a young boy in gray trousers and a green shirt had taken off his tennis shoes, rolled up his soiled brown jacket into a headrest, and stretched out on the floor. As he closed his eyes, the crowd, led by Hosea, began singing "Woke Up This Morning With My Mind Set on Freedom." In between songs the crowd would chant "We want Cohen." An elderly lady from New Orleans, who after the march obviously had little strength left to stand and yell and chant, simply shook her head in time with whatever she happened to be hearing at the moment.

The more pressure the officials put upon Hosea to relent, the stronger the support from the crowd. Given the demonstrators' vote of confidence, he began to rap. "I never lived in a democracy until I moved to Resurrection City. But it looks like the stuff is all right."

"Sock soul, brother!" the people yelled.

"Out here," he continued, "they got the gray matter to discover a cure for cancer, but can't."

"Sock soul, brother!"

Then, to the tune of the song "Ain't Gonna Let Nobody Turn Me 'Round," Hosea led the group in singing, "Ain't Gonna Let the Lack of Health Facilities Turn Me 'Round." And at the end of the song—something like three hours after the demonstrators had demanded to see Cohen—the word spread through the auditorium: "Cohen's on the case."

Demonstrators who had spread throughout the building buttonholing anybody and everybody who looked important, demanding that they "go downstairs and get Cohen," filed back into the auditorium. And as Cohen appeared, an exultant cheer rose from the demonstrators—not for Cohen but for the point that they had won.

Before Cohen spoke, Huitt came to the microphone. He looked relieved. "I'd just like to say, before introducing the Secretary, that I haven't heard preaching and singing like that since I was a boy. Maybe that's what wrong with me." The crowd liked that and showed it. "Get on the case, brother," someone called. And as clenched black fists went into the air—a gesture that had come to stand for "Silence!" and succeeded in getting it— Cohen spoke:

"Welcome to your auditorium," he said, managing a smile. He proceeded to outline his response to the demonstrators' demands, which included changing the state-by-state system of welfare to a federally controlled one. When he had finished, he introduced a very polished, gray-haired, white matron sitting next to him as "our director of civil rights." A voice of a Negro woman in rags called out to her: "Get to work, baby."

The second demonstration I attended was at the Justice Department. Earlier in the day, as rumors grew of dissension between the Mexican-Americans and the blacks, Reiss Tiejerina, the leader of the Mexican-Americans, and Rodolfo ("Corky") Gonzales, his fiery lieutenant, appeared for a press conference to be held jointly with Hosea and the Indian leader, Hank Adams. Accompanying Tiejerina and Gonzales was a small contingent of Mexican-Americans with unmuddied feet (during the entire campaign, their group remained in the Hawthorne School, where there was not only hot food but hot showers as well), and a few Indians. Tiejerina had one major concern: regaining the land in New Mexico that, he claims, was illegally taken away from his people some 300 years ago in the Treaty of Guadalupe Hidalgo.

As the press conference broke up and the demonstrators made ready for the march, the Mexican-Americans boarded buses to take them to the Justice Department, while the preparations of the blacks consisted of a black demonstrator's shouting: "Get your feet in the street. We're marching today."

The Justice Department demonstration was officially under the direction of Corky Gonzales. His demands were that the Attorney General speak with 100 of the demonstrators, with all ethnic groups represented equally— which turned out to be 25 Mexican-Americans, 15 Indians, 20 poor whites, and 40 blacks. The Attorney General agreed to speak with only 20 of the demonstrators, and this proved totally unacceptable to Gonzales. (Tiejerina was not there at the time.)

For several days, talk of getting arrested in some demonstration had become intense. Somehow, as the hours wore on during the Justice Department demonstration, it was decided that this might be the place. The question seemed to be, was it the time and was the cause broad enough?

There were some demonstrators who came prepared for any eventuality, regardless of the cause. As long as the order came from S.C.L.C. Ben Ownes, 52, widely known as Sunshine, was prepared. The crowd blocking the entrance to the Justice Department (a federal offense in itself), though led by Gonzales, was singing the S.C.L.C. songs: To the tune of "No More Weepin', No More Mourning," they sang, "No More Broken Treaties. . . ." Sunshine talked about his involvement in the movement.

"In Birmingham, in 1963, friends from my church were picketing. I went down. I didn't tote no signs, but my boss still told me when I got back to work not to tote. Then next time I went and toted. The third time I toted, I didn't have a job. But I'd heap more rather work for Dr. King for $25 a week than for $125. My house has been threatened. My mother has been threatened. But I registered a lot of people in Selma, Green County, Sumter County, and many others. Sometime I be sick, but I can't go home. I've gone too far now to turn 'round. I've been so close to so many things. Jimmy Lee Jackson got killed. James Reed got beat to death. Mrs. Liuzzo killed. September 15, 1963, six people were killed—two boys and four girls. If I die for *something* I don't mind. I've been in jail 17 or 18 times. But we really got to work in this town."

The police, however, did not seem to be in an arresting mood. They just stood in the street behind the demonstrators, more or less impassive. Suddenly Hosea took the bullhorn.

"Look at those cops!" he shouted.

The crowd turned. The cops shifted uneasily. "You see what they've done," he continued, his voice rising. The crowd looked. "They don't have on their badges, so that when they take you to jail and do whatever they're gon' do to you, you won't be able to identify them." The crowd was now facing the policemen and could see that not one of them was wearing a badge. Hosea started to rap about police brutality and the sickness of America. "Just look at that!" he cried, pointing an accusing finger. And no one had to be told, this time, what they were looking for. All could see that the shiny badges had been put back in their places—on the chests of the entire cadre of policemen standing behind them. But Hosea was now into his thing. "But look," he said, again pointing. "Just to show you how sick this country is—the sickness of America and racism—*look.*" The crowd was baffled. What was he talking about now? Hosea, virtually overcome with rage, now shouted, "You see how sick this country is? Otherwise how come all the white cops are lined up on one side and all the black cops lined up further down the street? Just look at it!" The division in the line was distinct. Immediately behind the demonstrators was a line of white policemen. To the extreme left of the demonstrators a solid line of black faces in uniform. Hosea rapped a good long while.

As the evening wore on, and the Attorney General did not show up and the demonstrators did not get arrested, there seemed to be some indecision among the demonstration's leaders. Hosea, at times, seemed at a loss. Corky had tired of leading the group in songs, and the demonstrators had never quite caught all the words. Corky and Hosea huddled often, only to return and lead more singing. Father James Groppi of Milwaukee showed up, received wide applause, made an impassioned speech, and joined in the singing. At one point, Hosea broke off to consult with his lawyer, and Tiejerina showed up. "What's going on?" he asked innocently. Hosea explained that the Attorney General had refused to see 100, but would see 20. "That's fine. O.K., isn't it? We send the 20?"

Hosea looked confused. "Corky is holding out for 100." "I will talk to Corky," Tiejerina said, and good-naturedly bounced off.

The evening grew longer. The demonstrators grew tired. Few complained, but many were curious. They were not getting the usual positive vibrations from Hosea, who looked haggard and weary. Then, suddenly, as if he'd blown in on a fresh breeze, there stood Jesse Jackson, who has been described as being closer than anyone else to Dr. King in charisma and in his acceptance of nonviolence as a way of life. Jackson was wearing a white turtle-neck sweater, and he towered above the crowd. Reaching for the bullhorn, he began, "Brothers and sisters, we got business to take care of." "Sock soul, brother!" "We got a lot of work to do on this thing, and we gonna march now on over to the church where they're having the rally to help take care of this business." Corky looked stunned. Hosea looked relieved. And the crowd of demonstrators obediently lined up and marched away.

The conflict between the causes of the Mexican-Americans and those of the blacks had come to a head. The relationship had been strained all along, but the S.C.L.C. and Tiejerina had kept it going in the interest of unity and solidarity. Tiejerina's lieutenant, Corky Gonzales, had demanded that Hosea support the demonstration at the Justice Department, and really didn't seem interested in much else. Hosea didn't mind being arrested. In fact, he wanted to be arrested. But this cause—the release in California of a small group of Mexican-Americans charged with conspiracy—just didn't seem broad enough. Corky thought otherwise.

Jackson was not only fresher than Hosea that night— not having been on the demonstration in the hot sun all day—but he was better equipped to deal with Corky, whose orientation was closer to that of the urban hustlers

Jesse Jackson was used to dealing with.

The around-the-clock demonstrations at the Agriculture Department were perhaps the most strenuous ordeals for the demonstrators. More people than usual were asleep during the day at R.C. because they had been up all night sitting on the steps of the Department. And they remained there, regardless of the weather.

One morning, as a weary group stood waiting to be replaced, the sky grew gray and a slight cool wind began to blow. As a heavy downpour of cold rain began, most of the group huddled together under army blankets and started singing.

The last demonstration I attended was on Solidarity Day. In that great mass of 50,000 or more people, I looked for the faces that I had come to know over the last few weeks. I saw only a few, and concluded that the veteran residents of R.C. just happened to be in places that I was not. Later, as the program dragged on and I became weary from the heat, I walked back into the city, expecting to find it empty. Instead I saw the people I had been looking for outside. J.T. and Leon and many others.

Harry Jackson, a cabinet-maker from Baltimore, sat in his usual place—inside the fenced-in compound of the Baltimore delegation. He was keeping watch over the two dormitories—women to the left, men to the right—and a frying pan of baked beans cooking on a small, portable grill. Since he was not out demonstrating, I asked him why he had come to R.C. in the first place. "We came because of the lack of association between the black man and the white man. If the system don't integrate itself, it will segregate itself all over again. Our group was integrated. We had one white fellow from the University of Massachussetts. But he hasn't been back."

This man, I thought, was probably typical of the majority of R.C. residents. They wanted things to get better, and felt that they would if people got together. The system didn't have to come down; it just needed overhauling. Still, the system had created the provincialism and distrust of larger communities that prompted Harry Jackson to remark as I was leaving, "I believe we should keep the people together who came together."

As I walked through Resurrection City, in the distance I could hear the sound of voices coming from the Lincoln Memorial—voices too distant to be understood. After a while, I ran across Leon and J.T. Leon said he was on the way to his A-frame.

"Why aren't you out at the demonstration?" I asked. And barely able to keep his eyes open, he replied weakly, "My demonstration was all night last night. Up at the Agriculture Department. And I'll be there again, all night tonight. That's why I've just got to get some sleep."

A few days later, Jackson and Leon and J.T. and every other resident of Resurrection City were either arrested (for civil disobedience) or tear-gassed (for convenience) by policemen from the District of Columbia. The structures came down in less than half the time it took to put them up. And Resurrection City was dead. Up on the hill, spokesmen for S.C.L.C. said they had achieved some of the goals of the campaign and were making progress toward achieving more. But the people were all—or mostly all—gone.

So, in the end, what did Resurrection City do? It certainly made the poor visible. But did it make them effective? Mr. Abernathy would have them believe that it did. And the people who believed him were, by and large, the ones who had come out of the same area that he had come from. An observer once said that Mr. Abernathy lived for the few hours when he could escape back to his church in Atlanta for Sunday services. This was home. Those who came out of that background were the ones who would have stayed in Washington until their leader said the job was done, working diligently all the while. But they, too, would be glad to get back home.

The confrontations of rural Negroes, not only with officials and the police but with urban blacks as well, may have engendered in them a bit of cynicism—perhaps even a bit of militancy. But one suspects that the talk, for years to come, will be of how they went to Washington and, for all practical purposes, "stood on Eastland's toes."

For the urban-rural types, who were in a transitional position to begin with, the frustrations inherent in the system became only more apparent. Already leaning toward urban-type militancy, their inclinations were reenforced by the treatment that even the nonviolent received when those in control grew weary of them and their cause.

The urban people did not learn anything that they hadn't already known. Except, perhaps, about the differences that exist between them and their Southern brothers. They expected nothing, they gave little, and they got the same in return.

Resurrection City was not really supposed to succeed as a city. It was supposed to succeed in dramatizing the plight of the poor in this country. Instead, its greatest success was in dramatizing what the system has done to the black community in this country. And in doing so, it affirmed the view taken by black militants today—that before black people can make any meaningful progress in the United States of America, they have to, as the militants say, "get themselves together."

October 1968

FAP Flop:
The Fate of Nixon's Welfare
Reform Proposals

THEODORE R. MARMOR/MARTIN REIN

It is now two and a half years since President Nixon presented to Congress his urgent proposal for welfare reform—the Family Assistance Plan (FAP). It is five years since Congress passed the 1967 welfare amendments in which the earnings retention rule of "30 and 1/3" was set down. And it is ten years since President Kennedy announced his commitment to "rehabilitation not relief." The three moves represent efforts to implement differing conceptions of welfare reform: 1962 calling for a service strategy of rehabilitation; 1967, a work incentive strategy; and 1969, a combined services, incentives and coercion strategy. As FAP evolved into the present bill, H.R. 1, coercion has come to be a dominant theme and legislative stalemate its fate. Yet, 7 percent of the population still receive welfare benefits and, in selected cities like Boston, 16.6 percent are on welfare. The most recent presidential initiative—1969 to the present—languished in Congress

with the ambivalent support of the president and the determined opposition of a powerful minority of congressmen.

The introduction of the Family Assistance Plan in 1969
was classic compromise politics for a Republican president
and a Democratic Congress: steal the liberals' thunder by
introducing a Republican version of negative income taxation; impose Republican party discipline in Congress to
get moderate Republican votes; throw sops to the conservatives in the form of slogans—"From Welfare to Workfare"; wrap it all up in the liberal reform rhetoric of the
past half-decade, concentrating on what's wrong with
welfare (which is very easy to do); and leave most of
the tough administrative problems to technicians or later
discussion.

It almost worked. Sixty-seven percent of those Americans polled after President Nixon's August 1969 welfare
speech approved his Family Assistance Plan. This plan had
two major parts. It called first for the federalization of cash
payments to a much-expanded eligible population—including all poor families with children—with payments based
on a national minimum income of $1,600 per year (later
changed to $2,400) for a family of four. Second, Nixon's
plan emphasized improving the work opportunity of welfare recipients through training, financial incentives and
supportive services (day care), all of it buttressed by
largely symbolic threats to throw off the relief rolls any
recipient unwilling to accept employment. The normally
conservative House Ways and Means Committee steered
the bill easily through the House of Representatives in
1970, adding restrictive frills to dress up the package for
conservatives.

Only in the Senate did this lightly glued package come
apart. In the summer of 1970, the groups that had for
conflicting reasons coalesced behind FAP found out how

much they disagreed with one another. Within the Senate Finance Committee liberals charged the reform was inadequate and inhumane and proposed as an alternative an income guarantee which was higher than the American taxpayer would likely be willing to support. The conservatives led by the soon-to-retire Republican Senator John Williams of Delaware, were skeptical of the plan's integrity, pointing out that the splicing of incompatible programs under the plan, when joined to other means-tested programs like public housing and medical care, left several glaring anomalies. "Work incentives!" said Senator Williams. "What work incentives?" And he proceeded to show that the Family Assistance Plan's formula for reducing benefits, in combination with the income testing of other government programs, entailed tax rates greater than 100 percent.

The outcome in the summer of 1970 was humiliating defeat for welfare reform. Nor did a liberal-conservative coalition capable of passing the bill emerge in 1971. The Ways and Means Committee tried to take into account the Senate criticisms of the 1970 plan, but failed to reconcile the contradictory and ineffective features of the original Nixon plan. Instead, President Nixon and the chairman of the Ways and Means Committee, Wilbur Mills, tried to keep together a coalition of supporters by continued compromise, satisfying none of the major antagonists.

The result was a slightly altered welfare reform bill, which the House of Representatives carried in June 1971 by a narrow margin, but the Senate defeated in committee. The reason for this pattern of passage in Ways and Means and defeat in the Senate Finance Committee lies not in differences in the committees' ideological spectra, but in the way they manage their respective conflicts between ideological groupings. Whereas the Ways and Means Committee under the strong leadership of Mills usually enforces a compromise upon conservatives and liberals, the Senate Finance Committee typically fragments on divisive ideological issues. Its liberals, led by Senator Fred Harris of Oklahoma, insist that welfare reform be generous and humane. The conservatives, led by Chairman Russell Long of Louisiana and including both Republicans and Democrats insist that reform "tighten up" welfare and keep in check what Long calls the "black brood mares of AFDC." In the middle, senators like Abraham Ribicoff of Connecticut, former secretary of Health, Education, and Welfare, remain committed to help those on welfare, and while they are anxious to avoid the punitive programs of Chairman Long, they worry that the result of too generous a bill will be no action at all.

And indeed, action has been minimal. The Congress did graft Nixon's "workfare" strategy onto existing welfare legislation: during the crowded pre-Christmas schedule it added mandatory registration at state employment services as a qualification for recipients in the AFDC program, an innovation which will have little substantive effect but much political appeal. The fate of welfare reform, however, remains uncertain. Meanwhile Senator Ribicoff and the administration have been engaged in a contest over substance and strategy. A flurry of tactical efforts recently drew attention again to the uncertain fate of FAP. Senator Ribicoff, angered by the Nixon Administration's failure to assist him, temporarily declared himself an opponent to FAP's enactment in 1972. Subsequently, Ribicoff worked out with the Nixon staff a plan whereby FAP would be "tested" in a few localities and, in the absence of a Congressional veto, enacted nationwide in 1974. In short, FAP flopped in 1971, a victim of legislative stalemate.

The Nixon welfare reform plan has reflected many of

the same dilemmas that characterized the old poor law, that is, how simultaneously to contain costs, reduce poverty and encourage the work ethic. Anxiety about rising expenditures and a dramatic rate of increase in numbers of recipients, and the pressure of state governors and city mayors seeking to ease the fiscal burden of welfare expenditures has forced the issue in the United States. Nixon's plan is a blunt instrument aimed at converting the present welfare system into a work incentive program which reaches the working poor and provides a family with a basic allowance determined by family size and family earnings. As earnings increase, benefits are reduced by some fraction of these earnings. In addition, the plan seeks to increase personal competence by training and supportive services and by generating jobs in the public sector. In the long run this strategy presumes costs will fall and the growth in welfare will abate. This is essentially the logic underpinning the welfare reform strategy. It is not a new approach at all, but a continuation of policies evolved since the 1962 amendments to the Social Security Act.

But there are inherent problems. The incentive system must relieve personal distress and reduce the fiscal burdens of states and localities. The more adequate the basic allowance at which economic insufficiency is met, the more demanding is the task of encouraging self-sufficiency. The more attractive the incentives (the proportion of benefits retained as earnings rise), the steeper the cost and the larger the program. How were these conflicts to be resolved?

The point is, of course, that they were never resolved. Consider one example. The administration was under great pressure from liberals to raise the basic allowance guarantee. No family can live on $1,600 a year. Subsequently the level was raised in 1971 to $2,400 a year for a family of four. If the original tax rate of 50 percent was accepted, a $2,400 basic allowance for a family of four and a $720 exemption permits a family to have an income of $5,200 before becoming ineligible for welfare. This contrasts with a cutoff point of $3,920 under the original FAP. Such a scheme has disastrous effects on the scope and cost of the program. Over 20 percent of the 52 million American families have incomes less than $5,520. An increase of $800 in the basic guarantee triples the cost of the program. Forced politically to accept the objective of reducing poverty, the work incentive objective was forsaken and the tax rate was reluctantly raised to 67 percent. The perverse effect of this change is to create a situation where the work incentive reforms already accepted as law for the past five years (because of the 1967 amendments) are more generous than the new reforms proposed.

Consider two other difficulties: one of the bill's major problems arose from the attempt to solve a long-standing anomaly in the American welfare system: namely, that the welfare poor have often been better off financially than the working poor. Hence, Nixon proposed expanding the welfare system to include the working poor. To do so and to raise the income guarantee at the same time require extraordinarily large budgetary outlays. As Republican Senator Carl T. Curtis of Nebraska pointed out during the 1971 hearings, a third of America's families would receive welfare payments by 1977 if the guarantee suggested by Senator Ribicoff ($3,000 per year) were law. Work incentives, equitable coverage, adequate income guarantees and low governmental costs cannot be combined.

To make individuals better off when at work also led to modifying the requirement that all cash recipients get an automatic passport to Medicaid, America's means-tested health program for the poor. The administration called for a new medical deductible scheme which works as follows: one-third of earnings which a family retains above $720 becomes the Medicaid deductible, that is, the amount of medical costs per year the family must cover before the federal government subsidizes medical care. Assuming a family had a $600 medical bill, the family would not be entitled to any subsidized medical care until its earnings equal or exceed $2,520. Such a scheme would leave present welfare recipients less well off than under the current Medicaid program in which poor families receive free medical care until their earnings make them ineligible for welfare. This results from the effort to reduce the value of the welfare medical insurance as income rises. Present recipients with some other income would receive less than the full Medicaid subsidy while at the same time no one would suddenly lose full medical benefits because of earning an extra dollar. The solution to this latter problem (the "notch") required graded benefits in health. Graded benefits mean less benefits if eligibility is not to be massively expanded. Thus efforts to eliminate some anomalies only produced others.

Another conflict has arisen over the preferred administrative structure for welfare reform. The classic reform goal has been simplified federal administration by a single agency. The model was an agency which distributed cash payments to very large populations—the Social Security Administration or perhaps the Treasury. The hope was that such payments would be made with courtesy, simplicity and dispatch. Or such was the dream of the reform economists who fathered the negative income tax scheme. Treating the poor in this way, however, conflicts with the administratively complex and costly task of separating the employable from the "unemployable" poor. The Ways and Means Committee in 1971, irate over the reluctance of

HEW and state welfare departments to make the work requirement programs work, insisted that families with different employment possibilities be administered separately. An employable adult member, according to H.R. 1, makes a family eligible for the Department of Labor program—Opportunities for Families (OFF). The AFDC program (at least for families with children under six) would be in a new division of HEW and renamed the Family Assistance Program (FAP). The complaint against the fragmented local-state-federal administration that had bedeviled the past has now been answered with a new set of fragmented federal arrangements.

It may seem unbelievable but the Department of Labor (DOL) is now planning a contract with HEW for cash payments to the employables under the OFF program. This splintering of responsibilities between HEW and DOL leaves unanswered the question of how persons shall move between unemployable (FAP) and employable (OFF) categories when their status changes (for example, the birth of a child). The pursuit of simplicity thus conflicts with the desire to categorize the poor for different treatments with respect to work.

Through all the debates, the one element of enduring consensus has been the call for state fiscal relief from the burden of welfare expenditures (the states now pay an average 50 percent of the costs of welfare). Under H. R. 1, 30 percent of the increased $6.1 billion in federal costs is allocated for state and local savings, according to the estimates of the Urban Institute's Jodie Allen in 1970. The Nixon Administration took up this banner in the beginning and conceded further relief as the states insisted that the federal government assume some of the costs above the basic federal payment of $2,400 per year for a family of four. In addition, when the states complained in

1969 that a federal freeze on payments for new AFDC families would bankrupt them, the Ways and Means Committee relented under pressure and removed the freeze.

The conflicts between fundamental reform and cost constraints, between the will to change and the requirement of keeping bipartisan supporters, were not candidly and openly admitted. Four programmatic goals came into sharp conflict—adequate relief in distress, effective, perhaps punitive, work incentives, substantial state and local financial relief, and reduced federal cost over the long run. The efforts to harmonize these objectives proved unworkable, and the problems raised were not clearly delineated. They were patched over, and the patchiness was revealed as special interest groups reviewed with the Congress one or another program feature. The patching arose from the Nixon attempt to win support from conflicting groups, from the effort to satisfy contradictory critics of welfare. As long as policy discussion focused on the need to structurally reform welfare, the underlying incompatibilities within the Nixon plan could be avoided. But, in the end, the bid for political support from ideologically antagonistic sides extracted its price: legislative stalemate after a promising beginning.

Instead of a program for all poor people, Nixon proposed one for poor families with children. That leads to a "baby bonus" for poor families without children; this woefully inadequate $1,600 to the present $2,400 and birth incentive worsened as the benefit level rose from the would be still worse if the suggested Ribicoff benefit of $3,000 were accepted. Ribicoff understands this and calls for universal eligibility in his amendments.

The efforts to reduce some anomalies only produced new ones. A program aimed at reducing rolls and costs must in the short run increase both; individuals are economically better off both at work and on welfare, since the wage system cannot assure economic independence for those in the low wage sector with large families. It also leads to new regional inequities in the implementation of work requirements, and there are doubts about the cost effectiveness of the H. R. 1 program when cost of training and child care are taken into account. In the meantime, states have opted to follow their own strategy of reducing rolls and costs—namely greater restrictiveness in eligibility and lowering of benefit levels. By November 1971, 20 states had reduced their benefit levels. Of the 26 states which acted, only Illinois and five others chose means other than reduced family payments to deal with the welfare crisis. Instead they used tactics such as more restrictive eligibility determination or more vigorous efforts to increase the federal share of state payments.

To convert welfare into an incentive system leads paradoxically to its further expansion and to a fundamental shift in the principle of making welfare residual by relying upon other, non-welfare institutions. The built-in contradictions and the changing political climate suggest that the incentive route is full of obstacles. A new direction is needed. And this new direction should be a return to the old direction—creating universal institutions for the relief of distress and the promotion of work. This would drive welfare to a residual role not by self-liquidation through the reform of recipients (training), but by the creation of new institutions such as public employment, negative income taxation and/or children's allowances and the expansion of existing ones, for example, long-term unemployment insurance.

The example of recent English reform is instructive. Older institutions—like children's allowances—have been revised, not discarded. The "claw-back" policy is basically

one of adding income selectivity to a base of a universal
system, but without stigma. The Family Income Supplement improves upon the eligibility of supplementary
benefits by extending a negative income tax to the working
poor. But it falls short of trying to liquidate Beveridge
social security measures in the service of a negative income
tax dream. America has yet to enact a "from cradle to the
grave" base; only then would its version of FIS—FAP
make sense as a partial solution to the problems of income
insufficiency among the working poor.

New solutions will also present new problems. There is
no final solution to the welfare dilemma; hence the simi-
larity between the issues of the past and the present. Still
in our judgment the logic of the present welfare reforms
is misplaced, and the strategy implicit in the original
social security act should be more vigorously pursued.

This essay has developed two quite different themes: the
political stalemate which characterizes America's efforts to
enact welfare reform and the anomalies and conflicts that
are expressed in the reform plan itself. The connection
between the two is political and causal, not analytical. The
underlying incompatibilities were accepted to avoid political stalemate. In 1970 there was a period when such a
weakened program appeared close to enactment. As time
passes, the forces which united tenuously behind a com-
promised welfare plan discover their differences even more.
The story shifts from agreement—the crisis in welfare—to
disagreement over what makes a reform sensible. Any
plan which becomes law this summer will testify to the
extraordinary gap between the Nixon Administration's
arguments for fundamental reform and the confused,
sometimes retrograde features of the plan they champion.

Two victims have emerged in the process. One is the
attentive reform public who have learned precious little in

two years of political maneuvering. American social policy debate moves like a turtle in a swamp. The other victim is the welfare mother and her family. In the major industrial states, real welfare benefits have eroded as reform attempts have floundered: AFDC families in New York now receive $262, $4 less per month than they received in 1968; in California, benefit payments have dropped from $212 in 1968 to $184 in 1971, taking into account price inflation. Some states retrenched as national champions of improvement brought forward their views. All states suffered from rising expenditures as reform attempts met stalemate. At the same time no serious efforts to deal with problems in the administration of the present program were made as the Congress participated in America's special preoccupation with simultaneously reforming and worsening the treatment of the nation's poor.

Welfare reform in the United States is many issues, not one. Politically, it presents many faces to a confused and largely unsympathetic public. The strongest constituency for reform are the states and localities, but their interest is in fiscal relief, not a reduction of poverty—unless their poverty is what is meant. Other interest groups vie with each other to define the issue of welfare reform in favorable terms. The Nixon Administration's political response to liberal concern for the relief of distress has been to increase the basic income guarantee over the past two years. Undoubtedly by summer, H. R. 1 will include a basic allowance close to the preferred Ribicoff plan of $3,000 per year for a family of four. The Nixon plan will most fully satisfy the persistent pressure for state and local fiscal relief by federal payment of a larger proportion of increasing welfare expenditure (the hold-harmless clause, for example). In the process, however, the work incentive hope of reform economists will almost surely suffer. Even now,

H. R. 1 has work incentive provisions that are worse than those provided in the 1967 amendments to the Social Security Act.

Welfare reform arose from the hope of converting welfare into a work incentive system. The politics of reform surrendered part of that ideal to administrative coercion and the realization of other pressing political goals like state fiscal relief. Attempts at coherent reform were stalemated, suggesting that to break up welfare—not to rationalize it—may be the only feasible long-term reform. What is clear is that confused legislation, embodying the compromises discussed above, will be enacted before the 1972 election.

June 1972.

FURTHER READING SUGGESTED BY THE AUTHOR:

"The Family Assistance Plan: An Analysis and Evaluation," by Lee Bawden, Glen Cain and Leonard Hausman, *Public Policy,* V. 19, No. 2, Spring, 1971, pp. 323-353.

Poverty Policy: A Compendium of Cash Transfer Proposals edited by Theodore Marmor (Chicago: Aldine Atherton, Inc., 1971).

"On the Origins of the Family Assistance Plan" by Martin Rein and Theodore Marmor, *Newsociety,* May 16, 1971.

Riot Commission Politics

MICHAEL LIPSKY/DAVID J. OLSEN

Speaking before the National Commission on Civil Disorders, better known as the Kerner Commission, Kenneth Clark wondered aloud about the usefulness of what the commissioners and their staff were doing. There had been previous riot commissions, Clark reminded his audience, and they too had issued reports. But the whole undertaking had, for him, an Alice-in-Wonderland quality about it, "with the same moving picture reshown over and over again, the same analysis, the same recommendations, and the same inaction."

Kenneth Clark's skepticism is widely shared. But should we despair with him that riot commission reports are ir-

This essay is part of a larger study of the political impact of riots on American cities to be published in 1973 by Transaction Books. The study has been supported by the Harvard-M.I.T. Joint Center for Urban Studies, by Transaction, and by the Institute for Research on Poverty, University of Wisconsin.

relevant? Or should we agree with public officials that riot commissions provide an invaluable service for helping society understand complex events? Or should we think cynically that riot commissions are no more than the tools by which chief executives placate and arouse people? These questions may only be answered by examining the place and function of riot commissions in the political life of the country. What do they really do? And how do they do it? How does one account for the great differences between expectations and results in the lives of recent riot commissions?

These questions open wide areas of disagreement, of course. But generally speaking, riot commissions are usually described in one or more of the following terms:

1. Government officials, it is sometimes thought, create riot commissions to provide authoritative answers to social and economic questions posed by riots, and to provide authoritative recommendations for preventing them in the future. This is certainly what commissions are *supposed* to do, as can be gleaned from reading the formal "charge" to any recent riot commission.

2. Others feel that riot commissions are simply a convenient way for public officials to buy time in which to formulate public policy. A harsher variant of this viewpoint has public officials creating commissions in a deliberate effort to evade political pressures and avoid coming to grips with the problem. A more sophisticated variant has the officials buying time so as not to have to deal with the passions *of the moment*. In the immediate aftermath of a riot, political executives have to conclude that neither the intense anger of blacks nor the intense fear and anger of whites are appropriate pressures or reliable indicators of what they should do.

3. It is said, also, that riot commissions are simply cre-

ated to exonerate public officials from responsibility for the situation leading to the riot or for their behavior during it. In the recent past a number of commentators have inferred that riot commissions have "whitewashed" public officials.

4. Independent of the validity of the above three positions, it is said that riot commissions are irrelevant to the political process. Essentially this seems to have been the position of Kenneth Clark in his influential commission testimony.

5. Regardless of the reasons for initiating riot commission activity in the first place, it may be said that riot commissions essentially function as interest groups, competing with other interest groups in attempting to influence the political environment in ways favorable to their general orientations.

In recent research on the National Commission on Civil Disorders (Kerner Commission), the Governor's Select Commission on Civil Disorder of the State of New Jersey (New Jersey Commission), and post-riot politics in Newark, Detroit and Milwaukee, we have tried to develop a framework for analyzing some of the above considerations. We conclude that formation of riot commissions gives rise to public expectations which cannot be fulfilled and that riot commissions are charged with incompatible goals which cannot meaningfully be reconciled.

Insofar as this is the case, riot commissions are most profitably viewed as participants in the ongoing political struggle of American race relations. They may make marginal contributions to that struggle by providing status and support for interpretations of riots which may affect the decisions of other political actors. They may also provide information about riots that will influence others, and may lend legitimacy to information which is already available. Riot commissions further may help structure the terms in which debate over issues relating to riots will be pursued. They are initiated by public officials as part of the executive function, but they are transformed by their constituents and, by virtue of the involvement of commissioners in commission business, they transform themselves into pressure group competitors in the political process.

But before discussing these points it will be useful to review some critical aspects of the Kerner Commission's operations. We will also mention related developments taking place in the New Jersey Commission where appropriate.

First, like other authoritative commissions appointed in recent times, the Kerner Commission was comprised of essentially conservative men. Of the 11 members named by President Lyndon B. Johnson on July 27, 1967, six were elected public officials, the most liberal of whom was Mayor John Lindsay (Republican) of New York City. Governor Otto Kerner, the chairman, was an Illinois Democrat known for his advocacy of both civil rights legislation and riot control training. Only two Negroes were named to the Commission, Senator Edward Brooke and Roy Wilkins, the most "respectable" of civil-rights leaders. The other members included Chief Herbert Jenkins of Atlanta, who enjoys a reputation for being a progressive among police chiefs; Katherine Peden, who was at the time Kentucky Commissioner of Commerce; and representatives of labor and business: I. W. Abel, President of the United Steel Workers, and Charles B. Thornton of Litton Industries. All of these people are either public officials or the heads of established American institutions. Indeed, as Tom Wicker wrote in his introduction to the Bantam edition of the Kerner Report, "President Johnson in appointing his Commission on Civil Disorders . . . was severely criticized for its moderate character." The McCone Commission, appointed by Governor Pat Brown of California following the Watts riot, and the New Jersey Commission were also made up of reputedly conservative people.

Second the Kerner Commission began its work amidst conflicting pressures for action. As the *Washington Post* reported, the establishment of the Kerner Commission "followed several days of congressional demands for an investigatory group either from Congress or the White House. Johnson was under pressure to act before conservative opponents in Congress created their own commission." It was quite clear that the thrust of these investigations would be toward discovery of "conspiracies" and techniques of riot suppression.

Third, the research strategy of the Kerner Commission was highly complex and difficult to implement. The President charged it with a number of independent and delicate tasks. The first was to describe accurately what happened in each riot city, and to do it despite an extraordinary diversity of testimony. Adequate handling of this task alone would have had severe political implications. The finding of a conspiracy, for example, would support those skeptics of recent black political developments who would like to discount reports of widespread discontent among black people in American cities. A finding that no conspiracy existed, on the other hand, would lead analysis into the tangled network of social causation in racial matters about which there is great controversy. The President also asked the commission to explain why riots took place in some cities but not in others, even though previous studies on this question had proved to be singularly unsuccessful. Finally the President requested proposals on how to prevent future riots. This may have been the most politically perilous charge of all. It demanded a review and evaluation of reform planning that would have to be convincing to (first) the commissioners and (then) the public. The peril lies in the fact that such a task raises questions of the capacity of this system to respond to social needs and the adequacy of previous programs. This diffuse research agenda had to be accomplished *in less than a year.*

Riot Commissions As Organizations

1. *The Scarcity of Time and Resources.* Such tight schedules are not peculiar to riot commissions, but the Kerner Commission and other recent riot commissions seem particularly hampered by these constraints. It is uncertain whether any riot commission could adequately fulfill the research goals with which they are charged. Almost as soon as commissions are convened, their directors find themselves confronted by critical deadlines. They must hire staff quickly without the luxury of fully assessing their qualifications and before the research agenda has even been completed. One consequence is that generalists, such as lawyers, may be hired over specialists, since staff directors may not know precisely what they want to do. The Kerner Commission was especially hampered because in late August talented people in the academic world were already committed, and because hiring had to proceed in the face of widespread skepticism such as that expressed by Kenneth Clark.

As soon as staff is hired, the pressure is on to collect the data. Investigation must follow quickly upon the occurrence of riots because of the need to interview witnesses while memories are still fresh and because proposed solutions presumably depend upon a research effort. The Kerner Commission decided to obtain information on riots in 20 cities, including environmental background features and interviews with key people, from city officials to militant civil-rights activists. The data-gathering teams went into the field at a time when December 15 was considered the target date for an "interim" report. This meant they had about two months in which to uncover the facts about the riots, the cities in which they occurred, and possible explanations for their occurrence. Obviously, this was too short a time period to obtain sufficient data to develop well-rounded studies, a fact confirmed by the Kerner Commission's decision not to develop all of these profiles for publication. The New Jersey Commission, given less than three months to hire staff and conduct and assemble research, was similarly constrained by time.

Another consequence of having to produce reports under this kind of pressure is that the staff is almost obliged to develop (or simply accept) a general working theory of riot causation to guide the research. The outlines of the theory are familiar to anyone who has looked into almost any recent commission report. It holds that systematic deprivation and discrimination in the past, when added to reasonable expectations of positive change and when accompanied by continued indignities and community resentments, become focused by a single incident or series of incidents into behavior that takes the form of looting and other hostile activities. As a general theory this is perfectly serviceable, but it hardly accounts for the varieties of civil disorders, which Presidents, governors and others are concerned about. Social scientists, especially, must find this unsatisfactory, since they are interested in explaining variation, rather than explaining why something does or does not exist. The questions of why riots occurred in some cities and not in others, or why riots varied in form and intensity, can be sensibly addressed only through a more rigorous comparative analysis than there was time to undertake in the work of recent riot commissions. Farming out research to social scientists was one way the Kerner Commission attempted to deal with research difficulties, but this was not entirely satisfactory.

As individuals with public constituencies, commissioners have to be assured that their decisions rest upon irrefutable and unambiguous evidence. The time problem intrudes when commission staffs anticipate these needs and try to "build a case," an effort that detracts in some ways from an open research strategy and diverts staff members from other duties. Staffers on the Kerner Commission, for example, had to return to the field to obtain affidavits from witnesses on whose testimony the narrative summaries of disorders rested. Staff investigators of the New Jersey Commission were required to file individual memoranda on every person with whom they talked on commission business. "Building a case" and good research procedures are not necessarily incompatible. But a strain is placed upon mutual satisfaction of both these goals when time is short. Statistics without relevance are collected; time-consuming procedures are honored to make an impression of thoroughness; theories with potential validity are rejected since they cannot be adequately tested, and so on.

Related to the demands for building a case is what happens when commissions begin to focus attention on the single task of producing the final document. At this point, other talents, perhaps antithetical to those of the researcher, are demanded of the staff. These are the ability to work all day and night, the capacity to absorb endless criticism without taking personal affront, and the ability to synthesize the sentiments of the commissioners, or to anticipate their sentiments regarding various issues. These qualities are those of lawyers, of advocates who work under pressure for clients regardless of personal interests or allegiance to material. In this respect commission staff-domination by

lawyers may be a necessary rather than an accidentally perverse quality of commissions. But the point remains that
those best able to gather and interpret socially relevant
data may not perform well in accommodating to the pressures that are brought to bear in writing the final report.

The pressures of time are also incompatible with a rational search for answers. Under rational procedures, study
should be followed by conclusions, followed by program
suggestions relating to those conclusions. But lack of time
required recent riot commissions to formulate their programs at the same time as they were analyzing causes. This
is not to say that their conclusions do not follow from the
analysis. But this dynamic helps explain why there need
not be a relationship between the factual analysis of events
and commissions' proposals for change.

Scarity of resources also contributes to the typical shaki-
ness of the organization of riot commissions. Commissions
enjoy no regular budgetary status, nor do they continue to
enjoy top executive priority after their creation has served
to reassure the executive's constituency that he has acted on
the problem. The Kerner Commission, for example, was
originally promised sufficient funds to accomplish its task,
but was later discouraged from seeking more money because in late 1967 presidential policy dictated seeking no
supplementary appropriations from Congress, and because
federal agencies were reluctant to contribute to the commission from their diminished budgets.

2. *Developing Commission Integration.* It is the peculiar
dilemma of riot commissions that commissioners are apparently chosen for the diversity of interests they represent,
while at the same time they are expected to agree on, and
support, a meaningful report about a complex problem
with clear ideological overtones. This circumstance sometimes leads the public to assume, quite understandably,

that the final report of any given commission will be little more than a collection of bland generalities, or an out-and-out whitewash. If it is the first, it will be because the commissioners were in fact representative of diverse and conflicting interests and were unable to agree on anything controversial. And if it is the second, it will be because they were really chosen by the political leadership for the basic congruence of their views. Either way, the appointment of riot commissions has led to rather unflattering expectations of their work, and often justifiably so, given the extent to which recent commissions have been made up of incumbent or former public officials and bona fide members of high-status organizations such as trade unions, financial conglomerates or the press.

Riot commissions are made up of men chosen for diversity of interests, and they are inherently temporary. Thus riot commissions are confronted in extraordinary fashion with the problems inherent in all complex organizations—the development of mechanisms of socialization and the development of group norms and values which may overcome tendencies toward fragmentation and disintegration. In practical terms, tendencies toward fragmentation and disintegration in riot commissions may take the forms of developing minority reports and developing destructive tensions between commissioners and staff.

For some commissioners, a minority report represents a threat with which, within limits, they can manipulate other commissioners to modify their views. The strong language of the summary of the Kerner Commission Report, for example, can be attributed to Mayor Lindsay and his staff, who in the weeks just prior to the final approval of the report had come to feel that the commission's approach was not sufficiently hard-hitting. Lindsay seized on the fact that a draft of the summary had not yet been prepared and had his staff develop one. He presented it to the commission as a statement of his position, indicating (it is not clear how explicitly) that he would issue such a statement anyway, if the commission failed to support him. The other commissioners, recognizing that the "summary" prepared by Lindsay reflected the report's contents, and that Lindsay might well release the summary in some form anyway, adopted it as their own. Mayor Lindsay's outspoken comments on the needs of cities may have had the effect of moving some commissioners toward his views in order to keep him in the fold. In any event, it is safe to conclude that the Kerner Commission summary would not have been so dramatic a document if Lindsay had not forced the issue in this way.

But, in a sense, a minority report is an ultimate weapon. One must still account for how commissioners with diverse interests and viewpoints come to identify themselves with the final product of a commission. Under what circumstances do such men permit themselves the luxury of political compromise in endorsing views to which they may not totally subscribe?

One way to explain the surprisingly provocative quality of both the Kerner Commission and the New Jersey Commission reports, given the essentially conservative cast of their members, is that their staff directors explicitly encouraged and engineered the development of *a sense of urgency* within these commissions. Direct exposure to ghetto conditions was perhaps the most successful technique to this end. Members of the Kerner Commission conducted two-day tours of riot areas, sometimes even without the company of the press corps or the guiding hands of city officials. One of the most successful of these took place in Cincinnati on August 30 when Mayor Lindsay and Senator Fred Harris, two of the most liberal members of the commission, met alone with a group of black nationalists. They were frankly informed of the group's dedication to the destruction of American society as now constituted. The confrontation apparently was particularly meaningful for Lindsay and Harris because the nationalists were highly educated men, and so could not be dismissed as being merely frustrated because of restricted mobility.

By the same token, the New Jersey Commission staff arranged for their commissioners to divide into teams of two and accompany antipoverty workers into Newark ghetto homes, bars and barber shops. Most participants, including chairman Robert Lilley, credited these tours with creating the sense of awareness and alarm about ghetto conditions that was ultimately reflected in the final report.

This facet of commission procedure in part was born of political necessity. Staff research was not immediately available to the commissioners, yet they had to demonstrate to the public that they were doing *something.* One way to do this was to study conditions firsthand. Happily, this also permitted commissioners to learn about ghetto conditions and agree on the nature of ghetto existence before policy papers were prepared and before it became necessary to "take sides."

Exposure to formal witnesses with dramatic testimony was also useful in creating a sense of urgency. Kenneth Clark's appearance before the Kerner Commission was considered influential in offering perspective to the commissioners on their activity. The same effect was produced when the staffs of both the Kerner Commission and the New Jersey Commission circulated articles by Robert Blauner and by Robert Fogelson that were highly critical of the McCone Commission. These articles alerted everyone to the potential public criticism of "wishy-washy" riot reports. Many New Jersey commissioners reported being heavily influenced by the testimony of black shopkeepers whose stores were shot up by New Jersey policemen; shopkeepers, after all, were not likely to be malcontents.

Problems of potential fragmentation threaten commission unity at all stages. Initially, the problem is one of getting commissioners to think of themselves as *commissioners,* not as individual politicians. This is helped, as we saw, by creating a sense of urgency among commission members. In later stages, the problem becomes one of conflicts arising from the fact that commissioners must begin to take stands on matters of public policy.

Considerable conflict did develop in the work of recent commissions at the writing stages, but these conflicts did not erupt to the extent that minority reports were filed or that serious public displays of conflict emerged in the press. The Kerner Commission did not break up over the appropriateness of criticizing major social institutions or over the ultimate tone and emphasis of the report summary, although these were issues of considerable conflict within the commission. Neither did the New Jersey Commission break up over the issue of recommending governmental consolidation for Essex County, although the commission was significantly divided over this issue. Commissioners clearly preferred to accept compromise rather than diminish the total impact of the report because of open conflict or sniping at the document. Members of both commissions have refrained from dissociating themselves from aspects of the reports, and many have actively defended them, despite the controversies they have set off.

Although there were considerable disagreements on the various commissions, what is significant were the areas of agreement. So far as we can discover there was little dispute over the causes of riots. The commissioners agreed that the riots were not results of conspiracies nor mass behavior dominated by criminal or quasi-criminal elements. Rather, these men (and one woman) chosen for their community standing and their connection with established institutions —people, in other words, who were relatively conservative in the literal sense—attributed the riots to long-standing factors of discrimination, deprivation and neglect. They condemned violence and criminal behavior, but they recognized that riots could be understood as products of central tendencies in American life.

There was also no question that extraordinary measures would have to be taken if the country wanted to deal seriously with the social bases of urban unrest. What debate there was concerned the kinds of measures that would have to be undertaken, and the kinds of criticism of American institutions appropriate for public discussion. But on the whole, these disagreements over the nature of the recommendations are less significant than the commissioners' agreement on the necessity for radical departures from existing public policy. When viewed in the light of the political and social legitimacy commanded by recent riot commissions, this is the significance of recent commission reports.

Apart from the danger of conflict among the commissioners, there is also the possibility of conflict between them and their staffs. In this regard, an important point of tension is the commissioners' need to feel reassured that staff members are free from bias and are presenting their work free from ideological distortion. Commissioners' suspicions apparently focus upon two possibilities. On the one hand, some staff members are feared to be overzealous for social reform, with a corresponding bias emerging in their work. This possibility is somewhat reinforced by the nature of lower-level staff recruitment, where an interest in social reform may be significant in the type of person willing to work for commissions on short notice. The field staff of the Kerner Commission, for example, was made up to a significant degree of young lawyers and returned Peace Corps volunteers. On the other hand, formally bipartisan commissions encounter suspicion that top staff members are really very partisan and have been selected to white-wash elected officials.

The dangers of failure to allay commission suspicions that the staff is overzealous or partisan are two: the com-missioners may reject staff work and in the end develop conclusions independent of staff analysis; or, in anticipation of commission antagonism, staff work may be screened to provide commissioners with only "acceptable" material. In either case, the commission runs the risk of staff revolt, the erosion of organizational loyalty among the staff and divisive public debate inspired by discontented staff.

The Kerner Commission was confronted with all these difficulties. The issue of staff political partisanship arose because some staff members were considered to have developed significant personal stakes in an "administration outcome" for the final report, and the selection of David Ginsburg as the commission's executive director did little to allay concern that the executive director would be fronting for the President. Ginsburg is a partner in one of Washington's biggest law firms, has extensive government connections, and was known to participate in White House social circles.

Openness and responsiveness of staff procedures, and symbolic staff appointments, are two strategies available to commission staffs in allaying commissioner fears of parti-sanship. The staff directors of the Kerner Commission and the New Jersey Commission spent a great deal of energy consulting with commission members about ways in which they wanted to proceed. David Ginsburg and Victor Palmieri, the deputy executive director of the Kerner Commission, were distinctly aware of the possible dangers of commissioners' suspicions. Sanford Jaffe, executive director of the New Jersey Commission, also indicated that gaining the confidence of potentially suspicious commissioners was one of his major concerns. In the Kerner Commission, the deep involvement of John Lindsay's assistant, Jay Kriegel, in commission activities contributed to alleviating Republican concerns over a potential "whitewash." The same could be said of the high-level appointments of Richard Nathan and Stephen Kurzman, both of whom had worked for Republican congressmen. Although staff directors of the Kerner Commission insist that these men were not appointed for partisan reasons, their presence was considered by other staff members to have helped reduce fears of partisanship.

Ideological splits between commissioners and staff are more difficult to control and can be quite damaging to ultimate commission influence. The prestige of the McCone Commission, for example, was severely undermined by critics who argued that the conservative cast of the commission substantially ignored the findings of its social science staff and consultants. The writings of Robert Blauner, Robert Fogelson, Paul Jacobs and Harry Scoble reflect this. During the life of the Kerner Commission, as well, major difficulties emerged over staff suspicions that their analyses were being rejected on conservative grounds.

The most obvious and best publicized example of this commissioner/staff tension revolved around the rejection of a document entitled "The Harvest of American Racism," drafted by social scientists employed by the Kerner Commission. From all indications, it appears that this draft was rejected for inclusion in the final report not only because its conclusions were radical, but also because documentation for its underlying theory of riot causation was lacking. There was also a problem of communication within the commission. The social scientists were shocked to find the document that they considered only a draft treated as a final product. This was devastating because the social scientists assumed it was clear that adequate documentation had not yet been appended to the theoretical analysis. On the other hand, the chief staff directors of the commission were no less dismayed to receive what they considered an unsubstantiated theoretical piece. The staff directors argued that for commissioners to accept a provocative analysis required, at the very least, that it be grounded in a solid evidential base.

Very shortly after the "Harvest" draft was rejected, the commission changed its timetable to eliminate the interim report and released most of the staff; about 100 people. For some staff members, these three events confirmed their suspicions that the commission was exploiting them without respect for their skills and was leaning toward development of a conservative report that was at odds with the staff members' analysis. Leaks to the press followed, and at least one commission consultant held a press conference to discuss these matters publicly. Thus, for a period in the latter half of December the Kerner Commission was under considerable pressure in the press to deny charges that it was heading in a conservative direction.

Release of the final report allayed these fears. Previously critical staff members now acknowledge this and, indeed, that much of their analysis was woven into the final document. By taking their fears to the press, these staff members may have contributed to the outcome by putting pressure on the commission at a critical time.

3. *The Development of Political Legitimacy.* Initially, riot commissions are charged with generating objective

analysis and impartial recommendations based upon this analysis. Initially, commissioners are recruited because of their status, their imputed objectivity and responsibility, and the extent to which they appear to be representative of a spectrum of diverse interests. We have suggested, however, that if commission efforts are to be successful, commissioners must give up some of their self and occupational role interests and develop orientations toward the commission as an organization with a life of its own. As this happens riot commissions adopt strategies to maximize the impact of the final report. We have already mentioned the example of staff directors formulating procedures to discourage minority reports. They recognize that a commission that appears to be substantially divided merely testifies to the complexity of the issue and is supportive of many viewpoints.

An insight into the efforts of riot commissions to develop legitimacy can be found in the tension between pursuit of a "scientific" research strategy (or "scientific" legitimacy) and the political needs of commission work (or "political" legitimacy). Staffs must conduct inquiries so that the commission appears comprehensive in searching for explanations and program proposals, reliable in presentation of evidence, and cognizant of advanced work in various research and program areas. This image must be secured by the staff for the commission whether or not information so obtained is related to questions or answers of commission interest.

Staff directors must conserve scarce time. Yet the staff directors of the Kerner Commission traveled throughout the country to demonstrate (as well as assure) that they had conferred with the broadest base of social scientists and were searching widely for expertise.

Moreover, mechanisms had to be developed to deal with

numerous inquiries from people offering their services (for a fee) and research findings. These inquiries and proposals had to be handled in such a way as to give the impression that offers of help were indeed welcome (when in many cases they were not). In this regard the Kerner Commission confronted a problem endemic to most government agencies. But unlike most government agencies, the commission lacked a routine for dealing with these inquiries, the staff to handle them or the time to evaluate them.

An illustration of this is the case of a prominent research-oriented psychiatrist who submitted his name through his senator, Edward Brooke, a Kerner Commission member, for one of the top research positions on the commission. He did not receive a reply until some months after the commission was thoroughly staffed. Then he received a formula response, thanking him for his inquiry concerning a "job" at the commission, but explaining that positions were no longer available. The man was insulted, and was subsequently uncooperative with the commission. The preemptory posture assumed by top staff members of the Kerner Commission of necessity, given the strain under which they operated, was resented in many quarters—both in academic circles and in staffs of subnational commissions. Especially irksome to the Kerner Commission was the fact that from the outset there was general recognition of the time trial the commission would experience; thus the commission was "marked" for exploitation by individuals convinced they could help, or convinced that the commission could help them.

Besides establishing their "scientific" legitimacy, commissions must give the impression that all political groups are given their day in court. Sometimes the motives for hearing certain witnesses are transparently political rather than educational or evidential. The Kerner Commission, for example, took the testimony of many of the black militants whose names appear on the witness list at a period when many chapters in the report already had been approved in relatively final form.

So far, we have been building an argument that the internal political dynamics of riot commissions can be characterized as the gradual development of a *pressure group.* This is particularly curious because, in the first place, riot commissions are established by public officials as objective instrumentalities to provide authoritative answers to questions of concern (thus, they are *government* organizations); and, in the second place, because riot commissions are specifically designed for the representation of *diverse* interests when originally formed.

Nevertheless, this view of riot commissions as developing into pressure groups may help explain both their strengths and weaknesses. Insofar as a diverse group of implicitly responsible, high status individuals subscribe to one interpretation of civil disorders and subscribe to a single set of recommendations, riot commissions may claim a high degree of political legitimacy. This is their strength. But insofar as a riot commission must compete in the political arena without being able to rely upon the organizational status of individual commission members, riot commissions enter an idealogical arena where they must compete with other groups in the political process. In that competition, the impact of commissions is predictably marginal. The executive who creates a riot commission assigns to it the function of authoritatively articulating goals for the alleviation of problems of civil disorders. But the goals become authoritative for the larger political system only insofar as they are accepted by other groups for conversion into public policy. In the absence of such acceptance, the recommendations remain only as political demands. They are purely recommendatory or advisory unless supportive relations can be established with interest groups and other key actors.

Riot Commission Strategy

In attempting to develop political coalitions and influence the political process, riot commissions adopt a variety of strategies to overcome their relatively powerless status. These strategies include: 1) maximizing the visibility and controlling the exposure of the reports, 2) competing for legitimacy, 3) affecting the political environment and 4) assisting the implementation process.

1. *Maximizing Visibility.* Riot commissions are concerned with creating favorable images of their activities, and attempt to do so by giving maximum visibility to their reports. The tone adopted in the reports reflects this concern. Both the Kerner Commission and the New Jersey Commission elected to develop what appear to be hard-hitting documents. In the Kerner Commission Report, as everyone recalls, "white racism" was identified as the over-riding primal cause of conditions leading to riots. This was sensational, assuring a maximum impact for the commission's labors. At the same time, however, the commission report contained almost no criticism of established institutions or programs. Criticism of national-level programs is largely lacking—despite the fact that the federal government is the only locus for the kind of effort that is called for in the report—and criticism is minimized of trade unions, big-city mayors and other groups who might be expected to do something about the alleged "racism."

The tone achieved by this report was not arrived at accidentally, according to a number of high-level staff members. The commission explicitly decided to produce a moral statement on the evils of racism and implicitly agreed not to specify the institutions perpetuating the condemned racism. Clearly the day-to-day interpersonal brand of racial hostility was not what the Kerner Commission had most in mind when it condemned white racism. The only way that white racism makes sense as a root cause of civil disorders is in terms of its location in and legacy for major American institutions.

The commission apparently avoided criticizing these institutions partly because to do so might destroy the commission's unity (those very institutions being represented on the Kerner Commission in the persons of business leader Thornton, Police Chief Jenkins, labor leader Abel), partly because to criticize these institutions would have involved the commission in nationwide debates with powerful organizations intent on defending themselves, and partly because the commission was dependent upon these institutions to put into effect their recommendations. Thus, criticism of past performances was apparently voided in the hope that future positive commitments might be forthcoming.

When it comes to manipulating the terms in which commission reports will be received and evaluated, the powers of commissions are extremely limited. The phrase "white racism," for example, which appears but once in the summary of the report, captured the focus of the press to a greater extent than any other single finding reported by the Kerner Commission. From a rereading of the summary, however, it would appear that the commission had hoped that national attention would center on the conclusion that the country was "moving toward two societies, one black, one white—separate and unequal." Similarly, the New Jersey Commission felt obligated to address the issue of official corruption in Newark because of repeated testimony on that subject by commission witnesses. On release of the report, the press, especially in Newark, gave a great deal of attention to the corruption issue, although it had a relatively minor place in the report itself. New Jersey Commission members indicated in interviews that they regretted including the corruption issue at all, because it tended to draw attention away from more important findings of their report.

2. *Competing for Legitimacy.* In attempting to influence other political actors on behalf of their report, riot commissions, as we have seen, try to establish firmly their claims as the authoritative interpreters of civil disorders and as authoritative planners for preventing future civil disorder. These claims do not go uncontested. Other groups have access to the same symbols and similar grounds of legitimacy.

Simply stated, one riot commission often begets another, or two or three. The competing riot commissions have less claim to objectivity or being "official," but they have greater claims to reliable constituencies and the group status that results. These constituencies are, for one reason or another, determined to undermine the monopoly of legitimacy asserted by the riot commissions and attempt to establish legitimacy of their own. They adopt the commission inquiry form in order to capitalize on the acceptability of this political instrument.

The political logic appears to be as follows: if it can be shown that opposite conclusions can emerge from the same kind of investigation of civil disorders, then it can be argued that the conclusion of the authoritative commission was the product of the biases of commissioners. This is all quite explicit, and antagonistic interest groups don't hesitate to use the tactic even when it is patently clear that the "competing commission" is undertaking a biased investigation. Take, for example, the remarks of John J. Heffernan, President of the New Jersey State Patrolmen's Benevolent Association, when he "predicted" the findings of his association's investigation: "We are appalled at the findings of the [New Jersey] riot commission, especially in the interests of law and order. The PBA riot study and investigation committee is certainly going to come up with different findings."

After President Johnson issued an executive order creating the Kerner Commission, the United States Senate authorized the Permanent Subcommittee on Investigations of the Committee on Government Operations (McClellan Committee) "to make a full and complete study and investigation of riots . . . and measures necessary for their immediate and long-range prevention." The McClellan Committee's investigations have attempted to undermine the findings of the Kerner Commission by centering on Office of Economic Opportunity personnel involved in riots, hearing witnesses who allege that there is a conspiracy behind the riots, and generally giving a hostile reception to other witnesses not sympathetic with the committee's more conservative views. That President Johnson himself tried to undermine his own Kerner Commission is perhaps not surprising. The fact that he included in his charge to the (Milton) Eisenhower Commission on the Causes and Prevention of Violence the duty to investigate civil disorders is consistent with his other acts of unsympathetic reception of the Kerner Report. The New Jersey Commission's "Report For Action," released in February of 1968, shortly thereafter triggered the New Jersey State Patrolmen's Benevolent Association's Riot Study Commission report entitled "A Challenge To Conscience." In Detroit, Jerome P. Cavanagh's Mayor's Development Team represented a public response to local civil disorders with most commission members drawn from city agencies and the mayor's office. But the Development Team was soon challenged by the New Detroit Committee, a private counterthrust to the public commission. In California, the conservative McCone Commission was countered, both as to its findings and its recommendations, by the California Advisory Committee to the United States Commission on Civil Rights.

These competing commissions employ many of the same strategies and tactics as official riot commissions in manipulating the symbols of legitimacy. They follow closely the procedures of the initial commissions, including assembling a staff, holding formal hearings, conducting investigations, hearing witnesses, collecting documents and offering recommendations. In fact, they are often the same witnesses, the same documents and similar investigations. But their findings and recommendations vary considerably from the conclusions of initial commissions. Riot commissions, whether initial or competing, thus represent ad hoc devices by which on-going antagonistic interests compete for political legitimacy.

3. *Affecting the Political Environment.* In content, commission reports can be analyzed as attempts to reassure various publics in an otherwise unsettled environment. These reassurances may take the form of dispelling popular rumors and myths, or they may take the form of interpreting disturbing events in ways that can be absorbed within traditional American beliefs.

Efforts to reassure various publics begin as soon as commissions are formed. Early testimony plays an important part in giving the appearance that significant interests are being represented. J. Edgar Hoover's statement that he had no evidence of a conspiracy was the only testimony released officially during the first set of Kerner Commission hearings. Then, as if to counteract the information that the chief criminal investigative official of the United States had no evidence of a riot conspiracy, Governor Kerner informed reporters that Sargent Shriver, Director of the Office of Economic Opportunity, and Robert Weaver, Secretary of Housing and Urban Development, both had evidence of the presence of unidentified strangers in neighborhoods shortly before riots broke out. In those days of crisis, it would appear that members of the Kerner Commission wanted to reassure the public that questions of law and order would receive high priority. But, recognizing that Hoover's testimony appeared to preclude a search for confirmation of a theory widely held by some Americans, Governor Kerner "scrambled" the first message in order to protect the commission from early criticism.

Beyond dispelling myths such as those of conspiracy, riot commissions also reaffirm traditionally accepted views of society. They uniformly condemn violence and reaffirm the principles of law and order. They also commonly invoke that series of beliefs in the American creed pertaining to "equality" and "integration." Note the concluding sentence to the Kerner Commission's chapter on the history of Negro protest: "Negro protest for the most part, has been firmly rooted in the basic values of American society, seeking not their destruction, but their fulfillment." Which values? Which America? The statement may have empirical validity when interpreted, but here it has primarily inspirational value.

Of course riot commissions cannot reassure everyone. Reassuring the black community that commissions are sensitive to their feelings about white racism risks arousing the anger of previously uninvolved white groups who violently object to this explanation of riots. Obviously this was the case with the Kerner Commission's focus on "white racism." The New Jersey Commission tried to reassure Newark blacks that their grievances had been heard and would be articulated in the commission report. But this intention was undermined by the controversial nature of its program recommendations. Half of the New Jersey commissioners argued that political consolidation of Essex County was the only means of establishing a tax base that would give Newark the resources to solve its problems. But other commissioners argued against consolidation on the grounds that this would, in effect, preclude the election of a Negro mayor precisely at the time when black people were becoming a majority of the city electorate. The first position risked disturbing white suburbanites upon whose support implementation of commission recommendations rested. The second argument risked reassuring Negroes of electoral success without providing the resources for basic services.

Riot commissions can attempt to quiet unreasonable fears, and reassure segments of the population that their needs are being addressed. But they cannot escape the difficulties that are incurred when controversial program recommendations are considered necessary. Recent commissions have explicitly chosen controversy at the expense of tranquility, but in doing so they have risked arousing political antagonists in the struggle over program recommendations.

These last remarks have been directed toward the more symbolic content of commission activity. More explicitly, riot commissions also attempt to affect the environment in which reports are received by treating gently the riot-related behavior of the executive, and by anticipating the needs of other political actors. Because of their relative powerlessness, commissions are dependent upon the favorable reception of their reports by the executive and other centers of power for maximum impact on the larger political system. However, these same political executives may have been involved in dealing with the control of the civil disorders and with programs related to the basic causes of the disorders. Thus the possibility is raised of commission's having to deal critically with the behavior of the political executives upon whom they are at least partially dependent for the implementation of their recommendations.

One drawback in exonerating the actions of the executive in civil disorders is that it gives credence to competing riot commissions in challenging the initial commission's claims to legitimacy. The New Jersey Commission strongly criticized the city administration in Newark. It left virtually untouched the matter of the governor's actions at the time of the disorder, which were widely perceived by the black community in Newark to be inflammatory. During the Newark disturbances, Governor Hughes had told reporters that he would draw the line between the law and the jungle, and that riots were criminal and unrelated to civil-rights protests. Naturally enough, city officials in Newark lost no time in pointing out the discrepancy between the commission's statements about the mayor of Newark and the governor of New Jersey.

Riot commissions also attempt to further their recommendations by anticipating the needs of other important political actors. The Kerner Commission at one point adopted an end-of-the-year deadline for its interim report in part to obtain consideration in the formulation of the President's budget messages. Later it adopted the President's "message on the cities" as a framework for some of its programmatic recommendations, on the assumption that this would appear to coincide with his legislative goals and thus receive President Johnson's endorsement. The commission also consulted with cabinet officers before releasing its report. This strategy was based on the erroneous assumption that the President would use the commission's recommendations as a tool for furthering his own domestic program.

4. *Strategies for Implementation.* It is appropriate to conclude by mentioning a number of explicit strategies that riot commissions adopt to affect the reception of their product in the political arena. Riot commissions have recently advocated extending commission life in one form or another. The McCone Commission, for example, chose this means for advancing its recommendations. Near the end of the New Jersey Commission's deliberations, a request was made to Governor Richard Hughes to establish an on-going review body including some members of the commission. A commissioner on Mayor Cavanagh's Development Team indicated that after the MDT issued its report, it was decided that an executive committee composed of the mayor and five of his top assistants should meet periodically to review what was happening to the MDT report.

The major drawback to this approach has been the lack of power of the commissions once reports are issued. If riot commissions themselves have relatively little power, then a few of the commission members meeting periodically have even less power in the implementation process. Paul Jacobs suggests that what the periodic review undertaken by the McCone Commission actually accomplished was "defending itself [the commission] against some of the attacks which have been made upon it," and serving a public-relations function. Governor Hughes never granted the request of the New Jersey Commission to be reconstituted as an ongoing review body. In Detroit, the Mayor's Development Team was able to continue meeting periodically, and since many of the members of the MDT were public officials, it was able to participate in the implementation process. The MDT illustrates another aspect to the commission paradox. Commissions comprised of public officials may indeed have power in the implementation process, but they will lack the reputation for objectivity on which their persuasive powers rest.

Commissioners as individuals have attempted to exert pressure on public officials for implementation. In New Jersey, for example, Governor Hughes was threatened by individual members of the commission with public criticism if he continued his failure to respond. Shortly thereafter, the governor and his staff received members of the commission and in an all-day session virtually wrote the governor's special message to the legislature. This message, which called for expenditures of $126.1 million on welfare, housing, education, law enforcement and urban problems, incorporated most of the commission's recommendations pertaining to New Jersey state government.

Functions of Commissions

Let us now try to evaluate the assumptions about riot commissions that were identified at the beginning of this essay.

1. Riot commissions are inherently incapable of providing sophisticated answers to the most important questions relating to riots. As government agencies limited in time, resources and staff, riot commissions can contract for a limited number of empirical studies, investigate the validity of some rumors and myths surrounding civil disorders, and make relatively intelligent judgments in describing riot occurrences. They can also make sound program proposals, though they must do so before critical research has been completed. Recommendations of riot commissions may be said to be authoritative in the sense that they are com-

prised of high-status individuals and are accorded high status by the fact that they were created by the chief executive. But their recommendations are authoritative only insofar as the chief executive moves to implement them.

To the extent that the chief executive fails to move toward implementation—as in the case of President Johnson—or to the extent that recommendations go beyond the scope of executive powers—as in the case of the New Jersey recommendations regarding Newark corruption—riot commissions must be seen not as authoritative but as competitive pressure groups in the political process. As such their influence is restricted to the legitimacy that they can capture and the political skills of individual commissioners who attempt to affect implementation.

2. It is rather fruitless to enter the murky area of the motivation of executives who create riot commissions. But our analysis does permit us to say a few things. Whether or not riot commissions are created in order to buy time, it is unquestionable that they do permit public officials to avoid immediate pressures for action and to postpone decisions for many months. Not only does the creation of a commission deflect pressures from the chief executive, but it also improves his bargaining position in a conservative direction by permitting him to claim that he is constrained by other political pressures over which he has little control. In the intense crisis following the riot, people seem to appeal instinctively to the chief executive for leadership. But the opportunity for decisive leadership, for making qualitatively different decisions about national priorities based on opportunities available only in crisis situations, may not be what the politician desires. Postponement permits the chief executive to wrap himself in the usual constraints of office where politics as usual will continue to obtain. Riot commissions also contribute to cooling of tensions by re-

assuring various publics in a symbolic way that their needs are being met. This may take the form of calling witnesses representative of various positions, making hortatorical appeals for justice and nonviolence, and so forth.

3. Is there something inherent in riot commissions that supports allegations that they are established to "whitewash" public officials? We may ask this apart from the question of whether some commissions are made up of members picked primarily for their unquestionable support of a chief executive. We think there is a built-in tendency toward the whitewash, to the extent that riot commissions minimize criticism of the public official to whom they must look for primary implementation of the report. Further, for the sake of commission solidarity and to avoid diminishing the report's impact by the airing of dissension, riot commissions minimize criticisms of institutions with which individual commissioners are intimately associated. To some extent, public officials attempt to influence commissions in favorable ways through appointments of political allies and "reliable" individuals to the commission. As we have suggested, however, this strategy will have limited returns because of the fears of partisan bias and the need to make the commission appear "representative."

4 and 5. Kenneth Clark's skepticism over the relevance of riot commissions is essentially justified. Riot commissions are not the authoritative program planners for a community torn by crisis and harvesting the fruits of past social injustice. Neither are they accorded the status that might accrue to them by virtue of the prestige of individual commissioners or the expertise that they command. Rather, starting from the myth that riot commissions will provide authoritative answers to questions of social concern, and that these answers will be widely accepted by politicians who will move to implement them, riot commissions move

through a process in which they become just another pressure group among many in the political process. And in influencing that process, their resources are insufficient to prevail in the competition.

The allegation that commissions have repeatedly come to the same analysis, recommended similar programs and failed to produce action is true, but as criticism it is misdirected. It is not the commissions themselves to which one must look to understand the "Alice-in-Wonderland" atmosphere that Kenneth Clark perceived. One must look to the political process itself—that greater Wonderland in which riot commissions play only a marginal role.

July/August 1969

FURTHER READING SUGGESTED BY THE AUTHORS:

From Race Riot To Sit-In: 1919 and the 1960's by Arthur T. Waskow (Garden City: Doubleday, 1966) is an historical and comparative study of race riots of the World War I period with particular emphasis on the Chicago Commission on Race Relation's investigation of the 1919 Chicago race riot.

Racial Crisis in America: Leadership in Conflict by Lewis Killian and Charles Grigg (Englewood Cliffs: Prentice-Hall, 1964) is a creative analysis of functions performed by racial conflict and of limitations inherent in Southern biracial committees.

Race Riot at East St. Louis: July 2, 1917 by Elliott M. Rudwick (Cleveland, Ohio: Meridian Books, 1966) is a thorough study of a major race riot including analysis of four separate investigations into riot causes and remedies.

Poverty Programs And Policy Priorities

MARTIN REIN/S. M. MILLER

The war on poverty is financially boxed in—on the one side, by the military priorities for the war in Vietnam, and on the other, by conservative domestic politics and assaults. In this state of siege, its progress is limited. But even if the conflict in Vietnam—and in Congress—were to end tomorrow, the anti-poverty program would still face major battles and possible defeat. For success in any program depends on strategy as well as resources. Given vastly greater funds and lowered political opposition, basic questions would still have to be answered: Which projects should the government support? How well are they planned? What can they realistically accomplish? What goals come first?

It is not the purpose of this article to recommend specific programs, whether old or new, which should be continued or started. Rather, we are concerned with helping to construct a workable framework for making such decisions—a framework needed under any circumstances of war or peace.

To set up priorities, we must consider what is wanted (values), what could be effective (rationality), and what is politically and organizationally *feasible*. We must not only know what benefits we seek, and why, but what we are willing to pay, or give up, to achieve them. Goals very often conflict; to promote one may not only mean neglecting others, but even working against them. Values must not be buried under technical considerations—the "whys" lost sight of because of the "hows." The kind of nation and life we think worthwhile—our view of the good society—must help determine the programs we choose.

There are no final or absolute answers here. Rather, let us explore what choices are available, how people choose, and how they should go about choosing.

Most programs for reducing poverty to date, whether in the planning or implementation stage, fall under six major headings: amenities, investing in human capital, transfers, rehabilitation, participation, economic measures.

■ AMENITIES. These are concerned with supplying services that strengthen and enrich the quality of life, that directly modify the environment of the poor. They serve as increments to personal and family welfare, whether as household help, child care facilities, or information centers. They extend the quality of living; if the poor have them, they are less poor in the sense of being without services. Alfred Kahn calls them "social utilities" and considers them as necessary as such public utilities as water and roads. They should not be considered remedies for a disease, but a normal and accepted service.

■ INVESTING IN HUMAN CAPITAL. Investment of wealth is a means of creating more wealth. Investments in "human capital" (an in-term among economists) concentrate re-

sources on making the poor more self-sufficient and productive: schooling, job training, health care, and various
techniques of fitting them into the job market. Theodore W.
Schultz believes that "changes in the investment in human
capital" are the basic and most effective means for "reducing the inequality . . . of personal income," rather than
such devices as progressive taxes.

But what is a good investment? The purposes of "investments in human capital" are not as clear-cut as the
parallel with investment in physical capital implies. What
purposes, for instance, are educational programs in the
war on poverty designed to accomplish? There is considerable confusion about this. In the nineteenth century,
the emphasis in the charity schools was on inculcating
character—good work habits and such traits as industry,
promptness, and reliability—rather than in teaching the
specific skills and abilities necessary to rise in the world.
The Job Corps and Neighborhood Youth Programs frequently seem intent on following this nineteenth-century
model. The rhetoric of these programs implies that the
goal is increasing lifetime earnings rather than conformity.
On the other hand, "good character" seems to be a pre-
requisite for higher salaries.

■ TRANSFERS. Transfers provide cash to the poor (and
to other groups in society). Devices include the proposed
negative income tax, fatherlessness insurance, children's
allowances, guaranteed income, and various cash subsidies.
They are a means of redistributing income outside the
market place. Cash transfers to the poor could be provided
in a way that promotes self-respect and perpetuates the
myth that they, like the farmer or subsidized industry, are
actually helping the country by accepting the money. Transfers emphasize a way to build up and assure total income,
instead of the 1930's emphasis on replacing income lost

because of illness, unemployment, accident, or old age.

But American public policy has been biased against the use of transfer payments to reduce poverty. We seem continually haunted by that legacy of Victorianism that a guaranteed income (for the poor) must increase shiftlessness, immorality, and illegitimacy. Subsidy payments to farmers or industry rouse few doubts about the danger to the moral fiber of their recipients. Public assistance programs seem less concerned with whether the poor get enough as the harm it might do them if they did. The prevailing orthodoxy (see Title V of the Economic Opportunity Act and the 1962 amendments to the Social Security Act) is committed to change sources of income rather than to increase it, to "get people off the dole"—Title V by work training and the amendments by social services.

■ REHABILITATION. This approach concentrates on changing people, usually by psychological means, to restore social functioning. It ranges from guidance and counseling, through casework, to psychotherapy and psychoanalysis. Rehabilitation hopes to overcome poverty by overcoming personal and family disorganization and deviancy. Those reclaimed will become more acceptable, more employable, more competent. Rehabilitation, seeking to change the person, accepts the environment as it is.

■ PARTICIPATION. Participation includes those activities that try to overcome many of the psychological and social effects of poverty by giving the poor a stake in society and a chance to affect their own destinies. As Alan Haber says:

> American poverty, while it involves considerable physical hardship, is primarily "social poverty." It isolates the individual from the social mainstream, denies him the respect and status of the "respectable" members of the society, and excludes him from mobility opportunities into positions of social worth.

But there seems a confusion of purpose. Is the primary goal and effect of this strategy to help the poor to help themselves, or is it a means to organize them so that they can exert collective power? Warren G. Haggstrom has emphasized the more common concern with participation as a psychological condition of powerlessness. Involvement "provides immediate and compelling psychological returns." But another interpretation comes from Richard A. Cloward: "Economic deprivation is fundamentally a political problem, and power will be required to solve it."

■ ECONOMIC MEASURES. One economic approach to reducing poverty uses the "dribble-down" concept—if production is stimulated and the nation prospers at the top, some of the benefits will also dribble down to the poor. Another approach favors "bubbling up" the poor into the economic mainstream by programs designed directly to benefit them—new jobs, more low-skill jobs, minimum wages, and so on. Which is the best way to promote economic growth and full employment? Some economists emphasize selective training for those jobs that are still unfilled and creation of special new job opportunities (for instance, nonprofessionals in hospitals and agencies). Others believe that the economy as a whole should be heated up so that a near-full employment situation emerges. But the concern with price increases, loosely called inflation, tends to stymie high-level employment, and many of the poor are low-skilled and not likely to be employed except with special inducements to employers.

To sum up, the six intervention strategies can be conceived of as attempts to change environment (amenities); to change occupational chances (investment); to change the pattern of claims on income distributed outside the market (transfers); to change people (rehabilitation); to change the distribution of power (participation); and, finally, to change the performance of the economic system (economic measures).

This inventory outlines not only a list of policy choices, but also embodies different conceptions about the meaning and causes of poverty. The different definitions of poverty imply different means to overcome it. What appears to be a concern with "poverty" is actually a tissue of sometimes conflicting agenda. The term "poverty" cloaks the competing objectives. We note six ways to describe poverty, beyond mere lack of money:

■ POVERTY AND SOCIAL DECENCY. By this conception, citizens have a right not only to freedom from want, which requires a minimum of income, but also to adequate (and not inexpensive) services. One cannot reduce poverty without providing housing, medical care, and recreation. The lack of these amenities is then, by definition, poverty.

■ POVERTY AND EQUALITY. Proponents of this view hold that poverty exists as long as the botton fifth (or tenth) of the population receives a shrinking or stable share of a growing economic pie. Their concern is with inequality— the position of lowest income groups *relative* to the rest of the nation. Improving the absolute level of a group without decreasing the gap between it and other groups may heighten its sense of relative deprivation. Improvement in absolute standards can lead to frustration and discontent, as the case of the Negro in the United States illustrates. Reducing poverty requires reducing inequality.

The goal of equity is not simply a matter of taking from the rich to give to the poor, but requires a searching way of examining the distribution of government largesse. For example, in housing we lump tax concessions with public housing expenditures as forms of government subsidy (as Richard Titmuss suggests), then we reach the startling conclusion that the major beneficiaries of housing welfare policies are the middle and upper classes. Alvin Schorr estimates that subsidies to the upper income fifth in 1962 were twice those to the bottom fifth ($1.7 billion to $820 million). Good housing therefore becomes simply a matter of equal treatment—the poor should receive at least as much from the government as the rich.

■ POVERTY AND MOBILITY. Poverty, according to this conception, is the lack of opportunity to alter one's income, occupational, or social position. In a rigidly stratified social structure, those at the bottom, even if above a subsistence level, are still poor: They cannot escape upward. Enlisted men in the armed forces are not in want, and they may receive amenities as a matter of right; but they may be, as William Grigsby has pointed out, nevertheless in poverty if they are forced to remain in a rigid social niche. Similarly the Negro—stuck at the bottom of the social hierarchy—must be considered poor even if he has an adequate livelihood. Whether or not children remain in the same social and occupational classes as their parents, therefore, can be used as a measure of the reduction of poverty and the rigidity of the social order.

■ POVERTY AND SOCIAL CONTROL. For many, improved income and services cannot be enough—for they are concerned with the social problems associated with poverty: alcoholism, delinquency, illiteracy, illegitimacy, mental illness. In the rhetoric of professionals, rehabilitation contributes to "self-actualization," but in fact it is more often used for social control—getting the poor to behave according to accepted standards. This view frequently merges into a broader concern with social harmony and equilibrium. If reducing poverty among Negroes did not eliminate race riots, the programs would be considered failures.

■ POVERTY AND SOCIAL INCLUSION. In this view, people are poor when they cannot participate in the major institutions of our society, particularly the institutions that affect their lives—that is, when they have little or nothing to say about schools, employment, law enforcement, or even welfare and other social services. "The meaning of poverty," writes Peter Marris, "is humiliation: lack of power, of dignity, of self respect. . . . It is a mark of inferiority, and so more damaging than want itself."

Some experts justify reducing poverty for economic reasons—the poor will spend their increased incomes for necessities and comforts and improve the economy; if the money went instead to the middle class, more would simply go into savings. Therefore, as the poor prosper, all will prosper. Humanitarian and economic goals coalesce.

But what if they should come to conflict? Then, to follow this concept to its logical conclusion, economic considerations must be given priority. We must prevent inflation even at the cost of preserving, or increasing, poverty; economic growth is more important than redistribution. At these points, the concern with the economy sharply displaces the interest in helping the poor or reducing poverty.

These different concepts lead us to at least three basic models of how to view the overall purposes of social policy:

■ ALLOCATIVE JUSTICE. Policy is guided by a commitment to the more equitable distribution of benefits—who gets what, where, why and how. This model emphasizes equal opportunity for investment in career jobs and education and for the redistribution of amenities, income, and resources necessary for well being.

■ POLICY AS HANDMAIDEN. This strategy seeks to promote programs that reduce poverty, but these are subordinate to other goals, such as economic growth, social stability, or physical renewal of cities. Thus, transfer payments to the poor could be primarily supported because they stimulate the economy. Or services and amenities to the poor could be aimed at reducing social unrest, providing a silent strategy for riot control. Or the major purpose of rehabilitation of the poor in slums could be to make them good tenants and to facilitate the relocation of those displaced by urban renewal programs aimed at increasing the real estate values of downtown areas. These programs are designed to win the joint support of what might otherwise be competing groups. But in case of conflict the secondary role of poverty policy becomes evident.

■ POLICY AS THERAPY. Many people, including a disproportionate number of the poor, do not behave according to our prevailing, accepted, and predominantly middle class standards. Poverty programs may exact conformity. Rehabilitation programs illustrate this approach.

This analysis leads to four fundamental policy questions. What are the purposes of the programs? How effective are they in achieving them? How feasible are they politically (what are the chances of getting them adopted and implemented)? How do we choose between competing desirable programs or goals?

The question of purpose involves much more than technical classifications. It includes value judgments about goals. For instance, do we consider adequate housing and health programs for the poor *amenities* (to make the quality of their lives more comfortable) or *investments* (good housing to prevent poverty, and good health to reduce unemployment and improve learning in school)?

It is a political question as well: Will legislators vote funds for an anti-poverty program unless we contend it will reduce poverty and crime or welfare costs? But a technical and rational question also is involved: What is the evidence that better housing and medical care will prevent poverty? Can we document the charge that the poor are really the most victimized by these insufficiencies?

Alvin Schorr has made an impressive and persuasive attempt to bring together evidence on the relationship between housing and poverty. He concludes:

The following effects may spring from poor housing: A perception of one's self that leads to pessimism and passivity, stress to which the individual cannot adapt, poor health, and a state of dissatisfaction; pleasure in company but not in solitude, cynicism about people and organizations, a high degree of sexual stimulation without legitimate outlet, and difficulty in household management and child rearing; and relationships that tend to spread out in the neighborhood rather than deeply into the family.

He believes that malnutrition, poor health, and inadequate housing reinforce each other in causing, and intensifying, poverty. As he sees it, it is not the "life styles" of the poor that disable them so much as the lack of means to live properly. What they need is not psychological or sociological analysis but health, housing, adequate incomes.

Others disagree. Their studies indicate to them that improved housing has little effect on such things as deviant behavior or physical illness. Nathan Glazer, for instance, challenges Schorr's assumption:

The chief problems of our slums are social—unemployment, poor education, broken families, crime. . . . Nor can they be solved by physical means, whether by urban renewal projects or . . . housing directly for the poor.

In fact, Glazer believes that social relationships have more effect on housing than vice versa; that broken families can nullify the effects of even the best housing. The facts Glazer quotes are impressive: Two-thirds of the poorest urban families (under $2,000 a year) do not live in substandard housing; further, most of substandard housing is not occupied by the poorest.

What about the traditional relationship between morbidity and poverty? Charles Kadushin concludes: "A review of the evidence . . . leads to the conclusion that . . . there is very little association between getting a disease and social class, although the lower class still feel sicker." That is, Kadushin says, the poor complain more about illness and stay away from work longer for it, but are not necessarily more ill.

Others challenge Kadushin's interpretation. Further, these data do not provide an argument against the development of health and housing programs for poor people. If health and housing seem unrelated, this may be because of difficult problems of measurement. Are the poor who live in standard housing overcrowded? Do they pay too high a portion of their income for this housing? They may be largely older people living in their own homes, while the families with many children live in substandard apartments. Inadequate statistics can distort the total picture.

Let us consider health in the same light. Even if morbidity rates among the poor are low, infant mortality is high, life is shorter, hospitalization longer, and disability has more severe consequences.

The fact is that we have so little good policy-oriented research that we cannot make any firm conclusion about the relationships between poverty and housing and health care. Consequently, we cannot be sure that better housing and health would help raise the poor from poverty.

But housing and health can be justified on other grounds than reducing poverty. Equality, as noted, is one. Inequalities and loss of dignity might be the crucial aspects of poor housing. According to Schorr: "It makes little difference whether bad housing is a result or a cause of poverty, it is an integral part of being poor." And the psychology of poverty is reinforced by seeing, all about, how the other half lives. By this definition, then, people without adequate housing or access to medical care are poor; adequate amenities reduce poverty. It is not that housing is instrumental to improved education or income; it is a goal in itself.

The second policy issue is effectiveness. What good is a program that does not accomplish its purpose? But, in the first place, what is a program's purpose? Anyone who tries to get a straightforward statement of goals from a social agency usually finds that they react as though their very reason for being were under challenge.

But if the agencies will not provide clear answers, what of social science itself? For instance, do present rehabilitation programs actually reduce deviancy? When the score is finally totaled, the answer turns out to be, mostly, no. Social science research generally winds up exploding myths rather than giving solutions. William Kvaracecous, who recently reviewed the literature on delinquency, has reached the gloomy conclusion that nothing works very well. Other studies support him. Social work techniques may make youths and groups more democratic, more willing to join in approved sports and dancing, but they have little effect on law-breaking. Walter Miller has concluded that delinquency depends largely on age and sex—young men commit most crimes—and therapy will not change these conditions.

Will rehabilitation and counseling help broken or ineffective families or reduce economic dependency? A number of studies—including the most recent analysis of a vocational high school by Henry Meyer—and his associates—indicate that intensive casework makes little difference in reducing social problems.

However, ineffectiveness alone is not always enough reason to abandon a strategy. A program can be effective in unplanned ways. Even if rehabilitation does not reduce pathology and poverty much, its ethical, moral, and humanitarian value should not be discounted.

Another practical political factor impedes effectiveness: We frequently adopt programs not because of demonstrated validity, but because they are feasible—we can get them adopted and financially supported. "It is always easier to put up a clinic than tear down a slum," Barbara Wootton argues. "We prefer today to analyze the infected individual rather than the infection from the environment." Rehabilitation as a means of reducing dependency has become a national policy. Also, for political reasons we have reversed the usual procedure by starting programs and *then* testing the concepts in demonstration projects. In such situations the pressure to find exactly the answers we are already committed to is hard to resist. Thus, what is politically possible makes a rational analysis difficult.

What of the argument that the poor should, as a policy, be encouraged to achieve power through collective action and pressure? Alvin Schorr has summarized the arguments against such grassroots involvement:

Efforts to promote self-organization fail more often than they succeed. . . . First, poor people have learned cynicism from bitter experience. They do not widely and readily respond to efforts to organize them. Second, when they do seek serious ends for themselves, they threaten established institutions or interest groups. At that point they are likely to learn once more that they are comparatively powerless. Third, the professionals who try to help them have, with rare exceptions, one foot in the "establishment." The ethical and practical problems that arise in their marginal situation are not solved simply by an effort of will.

The foregoing leads us to the third policy issue—the feasibility of programs that invest in human resource development. If we say that investment in education or training will result in jobs, can we deliver? Is there a coherent relationship between the learning and the job?

More education or training usually pays off in more and better employment. But how much education—and expense —before the payoff starts? College graduates are better off than others, and the income differences between them and the non-college population are expanding. But the differences in job opportunities and wages between high school graduates and dropouts are not great, especially for non-whites. They seem, in fact, to be declining. For males age 35 to 44 in 1939, dropouts earned 80 percent as much as high school graduates; in 1961, 87 percent. As more people get more education, the tipping point for education may come later and later. Investing in human resources may have a limited gain if would-be dropouts do not go to college.

How much education, how good, and how relevant to the job market are all important questions in job training. And on one or more of these counts most of our training programs have fallen down. A study of "successful" ex-convicts shows that only 17 percent were working at the trades they had learned in prison. Of 1,700 young people who applied to Mobilization for Youth for training, only "roughly one in four eventually achieved competitive employment as a direct result . . . ," according to Richard A. Cloward. And these were mostly for marginal jobs, paying marginal salaries. As Herbert E. Klarman says: ". . . in the past the market economy has apparently not absorbed appreciable numbers of rehabilitated persons."

The relationship between occupational training and unemployment is very low. First, whatever its faults, we have done a much better job of rehabilitating people than of preparing society to receive them; and training means little if it does not lead to jobs. The connection between jobs and training is frequently very loose. Second, our training programs are often simply not good or relevant enough. Cloward reveals that the youths who did graduate from the MFY program could not read better than when they started, and had failed to get skills that could qualify them for the higher pay jobs. Training just to improve character or work habits—the intent of many if not most training programs for low-income youth—is a poor investment.

Moreover, employers tend not to take this training seriously, or consider it a legitimate "credential" of employability. One of the great virtues of a diploma, or even an honorable military discharge, is that an employer will recognize it as a "credential" of employability and character.

Why train if that training is inadequate, discounted, or if no jobs are available? Real improvement can only come about with changes in our educational, referral, and economic institutions—which are untouched by the training programs. In short, unless relevant institutions themselves are changed, even highly promising programs will be frustrating rather than improving prospects. Training can be an effort to evade the issue of job availability.

Few people will argue that better training and more jobs for the poor are not desirable goals. But the stubborn facts are that most training is not good enough, and that the jobs which follow training are too often marginal or scarce. Education, to yield large payoffs, will need large investments. Are we willing to face these difficulties?

What happens when goals conflict, whether the conflict is real or apparent, recognized or ignored?

As Isaiah Berlin has astutely observed, there is a "natural tendency of all but a few thinkers to believe that all the things they hold good must be intimately connected or at least compatible with one another." In social policy, as in other fields, this is a delusion; goals often conflict, and we must decide on priorities. Here are four major areas of real or assumed value conflict:

■ PRICES AND POVERTY. Paul Samuelson and Robert Solow have concluded that a 5.5 percent level of unemployment is necessary to keep prices stable; anything less must result in inflation. "It may be doubted . . . that we can achieve both a satisfactory level of employment and price stability without major improvements in our antiinflationary weapons." Similarly, the British Labor government has recently discovered, with some distress, that if it strengthens its international economic position, it may have to let unemployment rise and renege on its promise to raise pensions.

In short, we may have to choose between social welfare programs and rising prices. As James Tobin says:

We are paying much too high a social price for avoiding creeping inflation and for protecting our gold supply and "the dollar.". . . The interests of the unemployed, the poor and the Negroes are underrepresented in the consensus which supports and confines current policy.

■ INCOME PLANS AND INCENTIVES. Raising incomes through payments can conflict with trying to get the poor into the labor market. Is providing an incentive to work more important than assuring adequacy of income? As Evelyn Burns puts it:

Workers whose normal incomes are very low and whose economic horizons are very limited may, if social security income is adequate for their modest wants, prefer benefit status to securing an income from employment, particularly if their normal type of employment is arduous or unpleasant, or if they are unmarried with no family responsibilities.

■ RIGHTS AND MISUSE. Support programs contain various

tests of eligibility, and provisions to punish violators. These are supposed to prevent cheating and make sure that welfare does not interfere with the free labor market and private economic incentives. These goals, however, conflict with those of economic costs and social rights. Obviously, the greater the gap between benefits and wages, the less effectively welfare can serve to increase demands in time of recession, and generally stabilize the economy; and the more rigid the rules and administrative control over welfare payments, the less chance of reducing feelings of powerlessness among the poor, and of establishing social benefits as legal *rights*.

■ ORDER AND CONFLICT. The goals of keeping public order and protecting the well-to-do and of safeguarding the social and constitutional rights of the poor often conflict. We have not only a law about the poor, which seeks to deal with their condition, but a law *of* the poor, based on police powers. As Jacobus Ten Broek has declared, it is "designed to safeguard health, safety, morals, and well-being of the fortunate rather than directly to improve the lot of the unfortunate." The goal is the protection of society against the poor rather than safeguarding the poor from an indifferent or callous society. When we encourage the poor to be militant and independent, to secure and exercise the legal rights to assistance and protection, we tend to sharpen this conflict. If they are to try to shape policy, they may become involved in boycotts, pickets, strikes, and other dramatic forms of protest—in other words, in threatening the "well-being of the fortunate." In such areas as school desegregation, the interests of the fortunate will be directly pitted against those of the unfortunate. These are natural conflicts in a pluralistic society.

Thus, the single, seemingly simple aim of reducing poverty hides the many and often contradictory goals deriving from different conceptions of what poverty is. They call for many different kinds of strategy, which cannot hope to satisfy everybody.

How do we establish rules to allocate limited resources to promote goals that are in partial conflict? Can we develop more effective methods of making decisions that specifically recognize contrasting objectives and give policy-makers a clearer choice of the costs and benefits of various combinations?

Cost-benefit analysis has become more popular as older decision-making methods have proven inadequate for fighting poverty. The economic market had long been the traditional way of making decisions—automatic, impersonal. More recently, politicians and their administrators have made many important decisions—reflecting the play of political and value preferences. But though it moderated some of the dangers of market decisions, political determination has brought new strains of its own—arbitrariness, and the obscuring of national needs because of political traditions and expediency. Cost-benefit analysis seeks to professionalize decision-making. It offers a rational, as opposed to a market or political (value) basis for making decisions. Means are in agreement with goals.

It makes important contributions. But it does not provide a mechanism for superseding questions of value and preference. When used that way, it has important defects. Our criticism of cost-benefit analysis is six-fold: It suffers from technical limitations; it can lead to a quantitative mentality; the issue of operational feasibility is largely ignored; it has no ready-made response to the basic question of what costs and which benefits; goals are difficult to delineate; and it does not deal with the issue of competing goals. The large-scale danger in cost-benefit analysis is that values surreptitiously and inevitably creep in. The covert handling of values limits democratic discussions. Nor does it, we believe, strengthen in the long-run an effective policy of poverty or inequality-reduction.

It implies knowledge and confidence about social data that are ill placed. One does not have to agree with the doubts that we have raised in this paper about the efficacy of housing or the connection between health and poverty to doubt that one can have much confidence in measurements of costs and benefits. Hunches are frequently more important than scientific determination. Obviously social science will develop and some uncertainties will diminish. But we cannot be confident that all our evaluations are based upon scientific proof and that in the future we will always have a firm scientific basis for choices to be faced.

Another technical problem is the question of the "interest rate." In order to calculate cost and benefits which are received or expended over a number of years, it is necessary to use some way to calculate future benefits in terms of their present value. Since present gains are valued more than future, the latter should be reduced by an appropriate discount. The level of the discount can markedly affect total benefits. For example, cost-benefit analysis of much vocational education would have different results if a higher discount rate were employed than in some present calculations. The appropriate level of the discount is not undebatable.

The result of looking at benefits over a long number of years is, therefore, inevitably an emphasis on youth. The longer individuals can benefit from a program, the greater the return. It pays then to concentrate on youth rather than on the aged. But are there not other reasons for concentrating on older workers?

Cost-benefit analysis tends to emphasize those variables that can be reduced to figures. For example, the inability in urban renewal to assign a monetary value to the aesthetic pleasure of greenery may be a serious difficulty. There is danger of sliding into the position that the only goals with merit and legitimacy are those that are quantifiable and convertible into money. Quantitative reasoning may lead to stressing productivity (return per unit of expenditure) over total results. Productivity can be high while total returns may be less than in some other kind of activity which has a high relative cost per unit of expenditure. For instance, it may be more "productive" to work with the highly educated, "cream" unemployed because it is easier to get them jobs than it is for the hard-core, long-term unemployed individuals. But which activity comes closer to solving the problems of unemployment?

Quantitative reasoning also tends to underestimate the importance of feasibility. Here we do not refer to the political issues, but to the effective implementation of a program. It may be that a particular program is highly productive with a likelihood of a return far outweighing its cost. But this program may be extremely difficult to mount because of manpower or administrative obstacles. Another program may have a much poorer prospect in terms of productivity and costs, but be much easier to implement.

In making these points, we do not argue that the defects cannot be remedied, rather that current practice tends to ignore them. But now we move into issues which are more basic to the long-term difficulties of cost-benefit analysis.

What is a cost and what is a benefit is not so obvious as it seems. To a large extent cost-benefit analysis narrows the definition of both cost and benefit. To what extent are second and third order effects of any action included in the analysis? This is largely a political and value question more than a technical one.

What is the goal? Our foregoing analysis has stressed

competing goals. Which should have priority is not only a question of rational calculations but of political issues and value preferences. Cost-benefit analysis provides some important kinds of information, but it does not resolve the issues of values, direction, purposes, or priorities. Is the goal to bring the poor up to a certain income level? Or is it a larger one of reducing inequalities within society?

Which is preferable cannot be determined by cost-benefit analysis alone. Cost-benefit analysis at best is only a tool. It may be useful, but it also can be misleading when assumed to have greater clarifying power than it actually has.

We must not be lulled into thinking that cost-benefit analysis can rescue us from choice. Three solutions—cost-benefit analysis, the marketplace, the political process—are probably necessary, but none is sufficient alone, or even together. Policy is not all about technical rules for implementing value-neutral hardware. No simple choices are on hand. The crucial issues remain: How do we define a good society? How do we implement it?

These questions must be confronted. Technology must serve purpose. There are several ways to reveal the techniques of policy-making as the politics that they are. One good way may be to create a pluralistic system of advisory planning where many interest groups have their own experts to develop and support their own policies. Herbert Gans suggests that this may have already developed in city planning, where a progressive wing concentrates on social planning and a conservative wing defends "traditional physical planning and . . . middle class values."

Value judgments have to be made—but who, specifically, shall make them? However it is done—overtly or covertly, consciously or unconsciously, democratically or dictatorially—it occurs. The planner is not a value-free technician serving a value-free bureaucracy. The assumption that politics is without content—only efficient or inefficient—is unacceptable. As Paul Davidoff says: "Appropriate policy in a democracy is determined through a political debate. The right course of action is always a matter of choice, never a fact." The search for "rationality" cannot avoid the issues of objectives and ideologies.

There should be many analyses, based on competing outlooks as well as assumptions. In a pluralistic, competitive society the people should weigh competing values, vigorously promoted, before they can make just decisions. But ultimately, after all technical analyses are made, the selection of goals and timing must depend on judgment; and judgment must depend on those brute preferences we call values.

September 1967

Reporting
on the
Social State of the Union

WALTER F. MONDALE

America's social goals were well stated by the writers of
the Constitution: to "establish justice, insure domestic
tranquility, provide for the common defense, promote the
general welfare, and secure the blessings of liberty for ourselves and our posterity." But in 1968 we see little domestic
tranquility; we see little justice for a substantial number of
citizens; and for millions—poorly educated, ill-housed, or
otherwise deprived—the blessings of liberty are a cruel jest.

The search for solutions to this modern dilemma leads
those of us in government to turn to social research. There
is increasing legislative hunger for social-science counsel.
Senator Abraham Ribicoff, in major hearings on the
urban crises, called no fewer than 12 social scientists to
testify. In order to improve the federal government's social-
science research capability, Senator Fred Harris of Oklahoma has reintroduced legislation to establish a national
foundation for the social sciences. He seeks to draw the

social sciences from the shadow of the National Science Foundation, thus giving them independent status and increased stature.

In government departments, a new kind of administrator is emerging. For example, Daniel P. Moynihan, former Assistant Secretary of Labor, is "one of a new breed of public servants, the social-scientist-politicos, who combine in their backgrounds both social-science training and full-time involvement in political activity." (See Black Families and the White House," Lee Rainwater and William L. Yancey, *Trans*-action July/August 1966.) Another new political animal in federal departments and agencies is the systems-approach expert, who—by means of cost-effectiveness analysis and other tools—seeks to help decision-makers understand all relevant alternatives and key interaction among them by calculating costs, risks, and potential results associated with each course of action. An example of this new breed is William Gorham, formerly of the Pentagon and the RAND Corporation, and Assistant Secretary for Planning and Evaluation at the Department of Health, Education, and Welfare, who has been appointed head of the Urban Institute, a government-supported independent research center.

The development of these new types of scientist-politicians suggests a governmental institution—an arm of the executive—that can combine a knowledge of sociology, science, history, social psychology, criminology, and social economics. These new specialists can place their knowledge in a governmental context, and bring a systems approach to bear on broad social programs.

Early last year I introduced in the Senate the Full Opportunity and Social Accounting Act, which was cosponsored by Senators Clark, Hart, Harris, Inouye, Kennedy of Massachusetts, McCarthy, McGee, Muskie, Nelson, and

Proxmire, who is chairman of the Joint Economic Committee. This legislation would draw the social scientists into the inner councils of the Administration; it would foster the use of the systems approach for an overview of the broad range of domestic social programs; and it would establish a system of social accounting to keep a constant check on our domestic social status. Furthermore, it would require a public report of this social audit.

In its statement of policy, the Full Opportunity and Social Accounting Act reaffirms that "it is the continuing policy and responsibility of the federal government, consistent with the primary responsibilities of the state and local government and the private sector, to promote and encourage such conditions as will give every American the opportunity to live in decency and dignity, and to provide a clear and precise picture of whether such conditions are promoted and encouraged in such areas as health, education and training, rehabilitation, housing, vocational opportunities, the arts and humanities, and special assistance for the deprived, the abandoned, and the criminal."

To accomplish this, the legislation would:
—declare social accounting a national goal;
—establish the President's Council of Social Advisers, comparable in the social sphere to the Council of Economic Advisers in the economic area;
—require the President to submit an annual Social Report to Congress, the social counterpart to his Economic Report; and
—create a joint committee of Congress to examine the substance of the Social Report.

In his Social Report, the President is to detail "the overall progress and effectiveness of federal efforts" toward implementing the policy of the act; review state, local, and private efforts to this end; and present "current and foreseeable needs, programs, and policies and recommendations for legislation."

The three-member Council of Social Advisers, supported by a staff of experts in the social sciences and in those natural sciences concerned with man and his environment, would be empowered to "gather timely and authoritative information and statistical data" and analyze and interpret them. The Council would also appraise the various programs and activities of the federal government and develop priorities for the programs, recommending to the President the most efficient and effective way to allocate federal resources.

The model for this act is the Employment Act of 1946, which has had an indisputably favorable effect on the nation's economy. This economic progress—owing in large part to highly refined economic analysis and indicators—is a powerful argument for using social analysis and measurement.

The Council of Economic Advisers recommends measures to maintain a stable, prosperous, and expanding economy. It operates on four assumptions:

—that welfare (the ultimate objective) is dependent upon the level and health of national economic activity;

—that economic factors can be quantified;

—that action by government can cause specific changes in the national economic condition; and

—that from analysis of economic data it is feasible to recommend specific action to achieve national economic health.

To do its job, the C.E.A. had to develop a system of economic criteria to measure the present and prospective conditions of the economy. It had to increase the expertise and the rigor of the economics discipline in order to reduce the margin of error in economic measurement. It had to develop tools of economic analysis, calling upon the entire community of economists for contributions. It had to proceed with caution so as to command the respect and acceptance of decision-makers. Finally, its recommendations and findings had to be action-oriented.

The same process is now appropriate and necessary in the social endeavors of the federal government. But we should mislead no one: This new job will be far more difficult. There should be no false hopes for instant success. For the most part, economic indicators are hard, cash-register data, and in most indices the dollar is available as a uniform measuring unit. Understandably, it is far easier to count the cash in a workingman's pocket than to measure the quality of his health or education.

A true attempt to apply non-economic measures to the quality of life in America could have a revolutionary impact on government. It might be the first time that government looked at the individual to see what government programs do *to* and *for* him—in other words, to discover the effect, rather than merely to measure the effort, of government programs. For example, we know how many people take advantage of Medicare, but there are no public reports on the quality of this care. The same is true of education, criminal rehabilitation, and much of the poverty effort (although the publication of studies on the effect of Head Start has been a laudable beginning).

At present, our social goals are vague and ill defined. The legislative requirement that the Administration deliver a public social accounting should sharpen the Administration's goals and social planning. This could promote setting long-range goals in, for example, education, health care, and the fight against environmental pollution, and encourage definite periodic progress toward their achievement.

Some argue that this system of progress reports will curb innovation and experimentation. But I think we have little to fear if we use fresh, imaginative ideas. And in fact, the lack of adequate indicators can actually conceal the success of government innovations. Critics of the Job Corps, for example, attack the cost per corpsman, while the Corps' effect on the corpsman's life and potential is ignored.

Some see a danger of the indicators' being manipulated for political ends, or the goals deliberately being set so low that accomplishment will appear spectacular. Of course, our political system is, at every level, vulnerable on this score. But there are checks built into the legislation. It provides for a Joint Congressional Committee empowered to probe deeply into the substance of the Social Report—to examine and criticize the declared goals, to question the philosophy behind the various programs, and to test the adequacy of the indicators . For a demonstration of how effective this legislative tool can be, we need only refer to the transcript of the 1967 hearings of the Joint Committee on the Economic Report chaired by Senator William Proxmire.

There are also other legislative checks on the Administration. The General Accounting Office has won a strong reputation for its auditing of Administration expenditures. Senator Abraham Ribicoff has proposed that this operation be expanded by adding an Office of Legislative Evaluation charged with "evaluating the results of the social and economic programs [Congress] has enacted." The Full Opportunity Act proposes to give the Administration new evaluative and analytical equipment. Certainly Congress should be given comparable legislative tools.

The Administration, with the program-planning-budgeting system directed by the Bureau of the Budget, is already taking limited steps toward improving program evaluation and the determining program priorities. And William Gorham, in his work in the Department of Health, Education, and Welfare, has been coordinating a panel working on a "social state of the nation report." No one can guarantee, however, that it will be a permanent institution of government.

As a matter of practical politics, the passage of legislation requires a constituency. Since most laws grow out of a need that has immediacy and relevance for a sizable part of the population, most proposed legislation has a constituency highly motivated to promote its passage. But where is the constituency of legislation that looks to the future—legislation that will have profound impact, yet is currently difficult to understand and in constant danger of being misinterpreted?

To build such a constituency, we must look to the social scientists themselves. And there are other allies as well. At all levels of government, social-welfare organizations and officials are concerned about the effectiveness of programs ranging from welfare to education, from city planning to health care.

The initial job in building a constituency is to bring the legislation to the attention of those for whom it has inherent interest. I have sent letters to 500 social scientists inviting their comment. Furthermore, editorials in media ranging from the *Minneapolis Star* and *Milwaukee Journal* to specialized newsletters have brought encouraging response.

The second step is persuasion, which in this case means education. Few people in policy-making positions are aware of the concept of social accounting—largely because literature on the subject is confined mostly to the academic journals.

The congressional committee is a useful educational device, particularly as an efficient information conduit to the policy-makers. The Full Opportunity and Social Accounting Act has been referred to the Government Operations Committee, which has sent it to Senator Harris's Subcommittee on Governmental Research. In the summer of 1967 that subcommittee held a unique one-day seminar to explore the ramifications of the proposal. Both that session, and the hearings the subcommittee held later, elicited highly illuminating views from social scientists, present and former government officials, businessmen, and journalists. Above all, the discussions buttressed the need for an institutionalized and on-going review of the state of our nation's social health, at the highest level of government as well as on the community and state levels. In great part the hearings produced more questions than answers, and exposed our ignorance rather than a wealth of information about social processes. But our country is now demanding the answers, and it is essential that we begin asking the right questions.

While the Full Opportunity Act will have a vigorous impact upon government, I believe it will have no less impact on the social sciences. There is every reason to believe that the social sciences—like economics since 1946 —will be greatly stimulated by enactment of the legislation. Such legislation may prod many social scientists into devoting increased attention to social problems that have specific relevancy to government. Instead of concentrating solely on research and comment, they will become active participants in policymaking.

Are social scientists up to the task? While most who have written me believe that they are, some are less confident. One social scientist of long experience warned, "The behavioral sciences, in my judgment, are in no real position at this point to give any hard data on social problems or conditions." He added, "There are many promises and pretentions; however, when it comes to delivery, what is usually forthcoming are more requests for further research. ... "

If social scientists have not developed the necessary sophistication to fully participate in policy determination, then they *must*—and very soon. For government at all levels is going to ask them for advice and value judgments. This responsibility is going to be thrust upon them, and I don't think they are going to refuse it.

I am encouraged by the reports sent to me by social scientists who are involved in both the planning and the evaluation phases of future-looking projects. The work of organizations such as Resources for the Future and the Russell Sage Foundation is well known. And, of course, virtually every major university has a center or institute doing extremely ambitious research on social problems. Others, such as the Center for Research on the Utilization of Scientific Knowledge at the University of Michigan, are devoting their activity to ways of using scientific skills in the social as well as in the natural sciences. The book *Social Indicators* (M.I.T. Press, 1966), edited by Raymond Bauer, shows how researchers can frame the important questions and meet the basic requirements for social accounting.

All this suggests that some social scientists want to become activists—to convert their role from that of observer to that of participant.

Today, because much valuable information disappears into the academic journals, many policy-makers remain unaware of its existence. A Council of Social Advisers could probably correct this problem by providing a funnel through which the findings of social-science research would be directed to government.

Of course, government policy-makers shouldn't expect a

full range of sophisticated social indicators to be developed overnight, nor should they expect evaluation and analysis that bear the stamp of certainty rather than theory. Scientific progress doesn't work this way. If I read the history of the Council of Economic Advisers correctly, it took that group many years, and experimentation by several Council chairmen, to evolve a satisfactory role in economic analysis and policy recommendation. This will be even more necessary when we are dealing with elusive social values.

Now, a word of warning: There is a history of mistrust on the part of some members of Congress toward the social sciences. This attitude is based partly on unfamiliarity, partly on poor communications between scientists and policy-makers, and partly on the fact that many Congressmen regard themselves as successful practitioners of applied social science—because they have won elections. Institutionalized channels of communication will help break down this mistrust.

Also important is the fact that policy-makers are wary of the political backlash contained in the findings of the social scientists. One dramatic example was the response of policy-makers to the Moynihan Report on the Negro family.

Finally, there are still a substantial number of people who see behavioral-science study as a trend toward the society of Orwell's 1984. They are wary of invasion of privacy in social research, and fear that data banks will make the individual increasingly vulnerable. These are legitimate concerns, often deeply felt by the social scientists themselves. These concerns demand vigilance. There must be guarantees against misuse of some of the most valuable equipment in social-science research.

But despite these difficulties, it is time to establish an alliance between policy-makers and social scientists. The alliance promises better lives and more individual opportunity through a more orderly approach to the future.

Of this need, former Health, Education, and Welfare Secretary John W. Gardner has said: "We have a great and honored tradition of stumbling into the future. In management of the present, our nation is—as nations go —fairly rational, systematic, and orderly. But when it comes to movement into the future, we are heedless and impulsive. We leap before we look. We act first and think later. We back into next year's problems by studying the solutions to last year's problems."

Bertrand de Jouvenel has written that the 20th century now has the opportunity to devise "a long-term strategy for well-being." As I read the Preamble to the Constitution, it seems to me that this was precisely the goal of the 18th century Constitutional Convention. Today, a vigorous program—backed by the collective political wisdom of the Congress and the technical expertise of the social scientists —finally offers us hope of achieving that goal.

June 1968

The Case for
A National
Social Science Foundation

Social science has had its foot in the door in Washington for some time, but now it stands a chance of getting its head in, too. Bills are pending in both the Senate and the House to establish a national foundation for the social sciences. The pages that follow indicate the range of testimony on S.836, the bill introduced in the Senate by Senator Fred Harris (D., Okla.). Harris is also chairman of the subcommittee on Government research of the Committee on Government Operations, and it was this subcommittee that held hearings on S.836 in February and June of 1967. A companion bill has been prepared by Rep. Donald M. Fraser (D., Minn.)

Senator Harris's staff is optimistic about the chances for the new foundation to be approved; the Senator himself is taking the tack that more money and recognition for the social sciences are not luxuries, but necessities. As he said in introducing the bill, "Man can accomplish so many things these days—not excluding world devastation—by merely pushing a button; we understand the button and the machine very well, but we are woefully weak in understanding the button pusher."

In the beginning, at least, the new foundation would do more for the visibility and influence of social science in Government than it would for social research. But this greater visibility and influence might end situations like those described by Herbert A. Simon of the Carnegie Institute of Technology: "Social scientists are . . . being handed problems whose physical, biological, and engineering aspects have been 'solved' and then being asked to take care of unwanted social and psychological consequences."

The endowment of the new foundation would be modest. Senator Harris has written into the bill a first-year authorization of $20 million. The National Science Foundation, out of its $480 million total, is already budgeting more than $40 million for the social sciences. The National Institutes of Health spent $39.5 million on social-science research this year. In all, the Federal Government will spend $314 million for social research in fiscal 1967. Of that, $239 million will be done by outside researchers. *All* Federal research—including research in natural science and about $2 million for the National Foundation on the Arts and Humanities—totals more than $5 billion.

Much of this research—in all fields—is nuts-and-bolts work, needed by an agency to do its job. The Department of Agriculture budgeted about $27.9 million for social research, the great part of which goes for studies of marketing, crop processing, and agricultural production—Agriculture alone accounts for about two-thirds of all Federal research in economics. The Department of Health, Education, and Welfare plans to spend $176.8 million for social science, much of it concentrated in applied studies in the Office of Education, but about $40 million to be spent in more basic research through the N.I.H. The Department of Labor devotes about $10 million annually to social-science research. The department allots $2.1 million for basic research, most of which goes for studies in labor statistics. The State Department spends about $5.5 million supporting social-science research and study abroad, most of it spent on the East-West Center in Honolulu. The department's Bureau of Intelligence and Research has an annual budget of some $4 million and produces about 1000 formal research papers and another 1000 informal responses to queries from within the Government. Its director, Thomas L. Hughes, characterizes this research as "more what serious journalists would produce if they had the time."

Much of the research done by the intelligence bureau is classified, of course, as is much done by the Department of Defense and other intelligence, security, and defense agencies. In some cases, the very existence of the research is a secret. The C.I.A. may produce more social-science research than all the rest of the Government, but no one really knows. (One informed estimate gives the C.I.A. about 13 percent of the 8000-plus social scientists employed by the Federal Government.)

S.836 prohibits the proposed foundation from doing classified research, but the original version did provide that the foundation could carry out up to one-fourth of its research at the request of Government agencies willing to provide the funds and relinquish control of the research. This provision was sharply criticized during the hearings, and Steven Ebbin, staff director of the subcommittee, reports that it will either be left out of the bill entirely or such research limited to nonsensitive agencies. Other changes in the bill, Ebbin reports, are that it will "carefully and forcefully spell out" that the new foundation should support training and education of social scientists, and that the foundation will be permitted to do research on the "state of the art" and on its own progress in supporting social science.

The bill itself is a windfall from the storm that accompanied the fall of Project Camelot. But the idea of massive Federal support for the social sciences has been around since the end of World War II. At that time, social scientists were clamoring to be included in the planned National Science Foundation, and they were included—under the umbrella heading, "the other sciences"—when the N.S.F. was established in 1950. Since the confusion between social science and socialism was particularly popular in those days, the backers of social science were willing to take what they could get. The *Journal* of the Americal Medical Association voiced a typical complaint against *any* inclusion of the social sciences: "The social sciences are themselves so young and their techniques at present so experimental and poorly controlled as to indicate some doubt as to whether or not their development has proceeded sufficiently to warrant incorporation in the proposed agency." Another professional group opposing inclusion of the social sciences was the engineers, but their point—in 1945—was that "the social sciences are important enough to be placed under a special roof."

Today the N.S.F. subsidizes a vast range of social research, but most witnesses before the committee maintained that its concentration is on the "scientific" wing of social science.

Although the hearings can be considered an exercise in macrograntsmanship, the social scientists who appeared were unfailingly frank in telling the senators that social-science research is bound to be controversial. As John Buettner-Janusch said, "It is very disconcerting and sometimes terrifying to read an anthropological or sociological account of one's own community." This prospect frightens the *New York Times* as well. "Could social scientists financed by the proposed foundation really work in freedom from fear of Congressional reaction to unpopular conclusions they might reach?" the *Times* asked. Harris, however, believes that social-science research can withstand criticism—and without the protective umbrella of the National Science Foundation.

This suggestion, that the social sciences might fare better under the N.S.F., emerged as one of the key points of the hearings. Harris's hope is that a new funding agency for the social sciences will promote more diversity in Federal research. And neither Harris nor anyone else expects the N.S.F. or the N.I.H. or any other agency to cut back on social-science spending on account of the creation of a new foundation.

However, none of the Government witnesses—even those favorable to the social sciences—made any distinction between giving more money for social-science research to the N.S.F. and giving more money to an entirely new foundation. This was apparently the result of a decision on the part of the Bureau of the Budget against supporting S.836. However, the Bureau has now been impressed by the support shown for the new foundation and is reconsidering its opposition. Perhaps the most significant co-sponsor of the bill, after all, is one who joined during the hearings—the former head of the speech department and a social-science instructor at General Beadle State Teachers College, Madison, S.D., a formidable fiscal conservative, Senator Karl Mundt (R., S.D.).

Senator Harris, it might be added, is himself by no means an enemy of natural science or the National Science Foundation. In fact, this fall he led a successful floor fight to add $20 million to the N.S.F. budget for fiscal year 1968 over the $480 million budgeted in fiscal year 1967.

The testimony below has been edited and condensed in order to present a picture of the concerns of the witnesses in a limited space. The full text is available from the subcommittee.

PUBLIC UNINTEREST IN SOCIAL SCIENCE

W. Willard Wirtz

I have tried to suggest what seems to me the issue before the committee by referring to the classic and now very tired statement of H.G. Wells: "Human history becomes more and more a race between education and catastrophe." My guess is that the text is still very good, but the times have very much changed the emphasis.

I am frankly not sure any longer, and I say it at the risk of being misunderstood, which side education *is* on. It seems to me that catastrophe may actually be the consequence of the disparate outcome in the race between two kinds of education—one in the physical sciences and the other in the social sciences. I believe that physical science may get so far out in front of the social sciences that a catastrophe may result.

I should like to emphasize that the present development of research in the social sciences falls so far short of its potential, and the necessity for its infinitely larger development, that our problem is actually one of whether there are ways to express a recognition of the problem. I have tried to grope for an understanding of something that, as I say, is so far beyond what we are presently doing that I am not even sure about the tools with which I am working.

I want to make it quite clear that this is not meant, in any way, as a criticism of the present scholarship in this field or of the present administration of it.

But I believe that there is a very definite limiting factor, and we might as well face it squarely. I believe that this limiting factor is a very real doubt in democracy's mind—but not in that of its antagonists—whether it really *wants* any further expert advice in the science of human relationships. For this is peculiarly an area in which every single one of us thinks he is an expert. And if he is not enough of an expert, he would rather play it by hunch than try to find out what somebody else's expertness might imply.

I do not believe it is much exaggeration to say that the present attitude toward social science—*real* social science—is just about the same as the prevailing attitude toward the physical sciences at that point in time when people looked and saw that the sun "comes up" in the morning and "goes down" at night and said, "Let us not bother any more about it."

Now, that type of mistake was so pervasive that it still characterizes our whole discussion about the social sciences. We got over that mistake, as far as the physical sciences are concerned, and moved forward several centuries ago—and particularly in the last 50 years—to a point where, instead of feeding the physical scientists hemlock, we suddenly elevated them to so high a pedestal that we are perfectly willing to recognize that they know a lot more about their area than we can possibly know. We have almost given up trying to keep up with them. And when they invent a new communications satellite, which involves consequences of infinite importance to the whole human race, we turn our franchise over to a corporation and just forget about the whole thing.

Now, we must not be tempted to do that as far as the social sciences are concerned, even though Kenneth Boulding of the University of Michigan—who always seems to me to identify what is just a little ahead of us faster than almost anyone else—has written:

"There seems to be a fundamental disposition in mankind to limit agenda, often quite arbitrarily, perhaps because of our fears of information overload. We all tend to retreat into the cozy, closed spaces of limited agendas and responsibilities, into tribalism, nationalism, and religious and political sectarianism and dogmatism."

IMPROVING FEDERALLY FUNDED RESEARCH

Dankwart A. Rustow

Let me sum up my objections to some of the current methods of Federal financing of social-science research.

Suppose that some recent international crisis has drawn the Federal Government's attention to the country of Ruritania. In due course, the head of some Government office—who has not the time to ferret out or read the half-dozen scholarly articles on the politics of Ruritania—approves a $250,000 research project on the subject. Contract specifications are then drawn up by minor officials in the procurement division, officials who have little notion of how research is conducted or knowledge obtained.

The money appropriated might pay the salaries of 10 first-rate specialists on Ruritania for two years—but it turns out that there are only three such specialists in the entire United States. And precisely because they are good scholars, they hold tenure positions at leading universities; can obtain private-foundation funds for their research; and hence lack any material incentive to take on a Government contract. Because they are good scholars, too, they are apt to feel repelled by the naive concepts and the clumsy jargon of the specifications.

The contract, therefore, goes to a second-rate or third-rate institution and to scholars who have little competence in Ruritanian politics. The additional staff that inevitably must be recruited will have even less competence. And whatever the research procedures followed, the results are likely to be far below normal scholarly standards. If some of the researchers are sent abroad, they will, in addition, make a bad name for American social science—and hence impede the work of the three bona-fide Ruritania specialists on their next trips to the field. With a bit of ill luck, they will complicate the task not only of social science but of American diplomacy as well.

If my picture is correct, it seems clear that no

amount of reviewing of contracts by officials in the State Department's Bureau of Intelligence and Research will safeguard against these dangers. On the contrary, the additional paperwork and negotiation involved is likely to keep good scholars further away from Government projects.

Let me emphasize that the evils I see are not caused type of procedure that I have tried to describe. The dangers can be avoided, and opportunities for high-quality research can be maximized, I believe, by adopting three principles for all Government-sponsored basic research in the social sciences.

■ The initiative for the formulation of research projects must come from the scholarly side.

■ The allocation of funds for research proposals must be in the hands of groups of people who are themselves well-qualified social scientists and experienced researchers.

■ There should be an emphasis on projects by individuals, by small groups, or by established institutions, rather than by far-flung organizations set up *ad hoc.*

I hasten to add that there are several programs under military or partially military sponsorship that have, in effect, worked on those principles in the past—the work of the Russian Research Center at Harvard, of the Center of International Studies at the Massachusetts Institute of Technology, and of the Social Science Division of the RAND Corporation being prominent examples. These organizations have consisted of first-rate scholars; their work has not been dependent wholly on Government funds; and their prestige has been such that, in any negotiations for contracts with Government agencies, it was their collective scholarly judgment— rather than some uninformed bureaucratic judgment—

that could prevail. But I submit that these have been rather exceptional cases, and that the operations and vicissitudes of Project Camelot have perhaps been more typical of what one has a right to expect of militarily-sponsored social science.

A "MAJOR STEP" IN AMERICA'S PROGRESS

Fred Harvey Harrington

In reviewing the February testimony before this committee on S.836, and the hearings last summer on international science and behavioral research, I was struck with the feeling that, in many respects, the social sciences are today where the physical and biological sciences were in the late 1940s. At that time my predecessors in the presidency of the University of Wisconsin—Edwin B. Fred and the late Conrad Elvehjem—came here to plead for the creation of the National Science Foundation.

They described, for example, how university scientists had labored for years in fundamental studies of the atom—useless information at the time—and how in the dead of night in World War II, after the possible application of this "pursuit of knowledge for its own sake" had been recognized, Wisconsin's atom smasher was moved from the campus to Los Alamos. They called for postwar rebuilding of the "stockpile of basic scientific knowledge" that fuels economic and industrial progress and improvements in public health. They complained that Government agencies—conscious of their legal goals—concentrated their grants in problem-solving studies and areas where fast answers were needed. They warned that this was short-sighted, that the Federal Government was responsible for building both the strength of the scientific community and the store of fundamental knowledge, and that if this was left undone the nation would suffer. Science must have a spokesman at the highest administrative councils, they said. The need for fundamental studies must be understood and funded.

My points to you today are virtually the same—but for the social sciences.

As long as there have been scholars in history, economics, political science, sociology, communication, and the other social studies, there has been fundamental research in these areas. All major universities in America recognize the distinctive characteristics of the social sciences and tend to hold them together in recognition of their status with the biological and physical sciences, the arts and the humanities. In some respects they are the bridge between C.P. Snow's two cultures, the reason why American universities do not have the great, impassable chasm he so dramatically described.

That we look today to the social sciences for answers to our problems of poverty, international development, urban sprawl, and all the other social, economic, and political ills that man is heir to is evidence enough of the importance of the social sciences to the nation. But the pressing nature of these problems has developed public impatience with the scholar who says, "We must know more about man and his institutions and interrelationships before we can come to long-range solutions."

Obviously, in the physical and biological sciences, as well as in the social sciences, both applied and fundamental work must go on simultaneously. A national foundation for the social sciences can make this possible, as did the National Science Foundation.

There are some who contend that these things could be accomplished within the present Federal structure—that social sciences, as half-brother to the natural sciences on the one side and to the humanities on the other, could prosper. It is too early in the life of the National Foundation for the Arts and Humanities to ask that it produce some evidence of fair treatment of its half-brother. But the N.S.F., sincere in its efforts to spread its concern into the social sciences, has not yet proved, with a $21-million expenditure, its effectiveness in invigorating fundamental social studies.

There are some who contend that the creation of a third foundation would destroy the unity of knowledge or impair the interrelationship of scholars in the various fields. Quite the contrary, it would remove a source of irritation and improve interrelationships and inter-disciplinary research efforts. There is no one so irrationally irritating at a family reunion as a poor relative. Raising the status and the funding of the social sciences would enhance the unity of knowledge.

There are some who contend that adding another foundation would fragment Governmental support of fundamental research. And it would—to the benefit of all. It would place in the hands of a social-scientist administrator and a board of social scientists a considerable amount of responsibility for the progress in the social sciences. There may be some evil in this, but it is nothing compared with the suspicions spawned when this responsibility falls upon an administrator who is a physicist and a board heavily weighted with physical and biological scientists, regardless of their good intentions.

There are some who contend that establishment of a foundation for the social sciences might reduce the support from other Federal agencies for social-science research. This is possible, and may also be helpful. The creation of the N.S.F. reduced appreciably the "bootlegging" of fundamental study support into project work in the natural sciences. The creation of a social-science foundation could be expected to have similar results. And this could bring some reason and regularity into the whole field of Federal research support.

I do have a recommendation for change in S.836, a change I consider extremely important.

Americans like to see quick results from expenditures of tax dollars, and I don't blame them. We ask a great deal of our people. But by its very nature, a national foundation for the social sciences will not produce quick results. And by the modest appropriation proposed, the possibility of major, fast advance through the studies it supports is extremely limited.

The expenditures for social-science studies at the University of Wisconsin are currently about $8 million a year. With this volume of work, we produce few spectacular findings. Thus I would strongly recommend that you raise the fiscal sights of this bill to a point so that significant, early progress is likely. My personal feeling is that this could be accomplished with an annual appropriation of $500 million at the start, with a provision for raises over the years at the rate of about 10 percent a year.

This is a small percentage of our nation's annual investment in the *repair* of social damage. Prevention is always cheaper than a cure.

In addition, I see in the creation of a national foundation for the social sciences a major step in the progress of America toward a good life for all its people and an approach to world peace and fellowship. We should not quibble when the goals are of such magnitude.

WHO USES U.S.-SPONSORED RESEARCH?

John M. Plank

Government-sponsored research in the social sciences that is done on the outside can be ranged along a number of spectra. The principal spectrum is the one running from basic research at one end to something not far removed from spot intelligence at the other. And it is with that spectrum that I want to deal here.

In terms of content, it is impossible to draw a hard-and-fast line between intelligence and research, a fact given implicit recognition in the very title of the State Department "Bureau of Intelligence and Research." A good social-science research product will contain much valuable intelligence material, and a good spot-intelligence report often contains information of substantial research value.

As seen by the U.S. Government, both intelligence and research reports are designed for the same end-users, the policy-makers, to help them function better. As seen by the outside research world, however, the distinction between intelligence and research is felt to be a real one, intelligence being somehow unsavory, arcane, vaguely pernicious, and research being the opposite of these things.

I believe the research community is profoundly mistaken about the nature of intelligence and that it should reexamine its attitude. On the other hand, the propensity of those in government to classify their data as secret, to force outsiders who would deal with these data to go through elaborate rites of initiation— clearances, interrogations, and briefings—and, in general, to divide the citizenry into "insiders" and "outsiders," discourages really effective communication and cooperation between the two worlds.

In any event, it seems to me that classification is carried much too far, and that most of the outside research in the social sciences presently contracted for by individual Government agencies could be supported —more efficiently, more effectively, and less hazardously—by a single national social-sciences foundation. This is emphatically true of such massive basic-research projects as the unfortunate Camelot; it is true, also, in my view, of most studies of groups, institutions, and trends. Two points in this connection:

■ I strongly suspect that the ideas for most external research projects do not originate inside the funding agencies, but on the outside. Sometimes a full-fledged project proposal will be submitted by an outside researcher to a potential funding agency inside government. Sometimes the idea for a project will emerge during a conversation between a Government representative and an outsider. Sometimes a Government officer will come across the germ of a research project in his reading of what in the State Department is called "collateral" material—anything not prepared under official auspices. I suspect it is in such ways that most external research projects originate, rather than through intensive in-house planning.

My judgment is that a well-staffed, alert national foundation for the social sciences would elicit as good, or better, research proposals in as great, or greater, quantity from the outside-research community as the individual Government agencies do today. My further judgment is that those projects, when carried out, would prove to be of as great, or greater, usefulness to the operating agencies as the products of the present system.

■ I think we need to ask what use is now made inside government of the products of external social-science research. Who reads the results of this research? Who makes policy on the basis of an understanding of it? There are, as we know, mountains of such research in the State Department, the Defense Department, the Central Intelligence Agency, and elsewhere. My own observation is that comparatively little use is made of it—partly because most of it does not lend itself to direct and immediate policy proposals, and partly because people in policy-making positions in government simply do not have the time, the energy, or even perhaps the background to assimilate it and draw operationally useful conclusions.

What I am suggesting is that much of the present external-research product is not being fully exploited. And I think it is likely that shifting the source of funding for basic research in the social sciences, and publishing all such research, would not radically affect either the policy-making machinery of government or the nature of the policy made. Indeed, much research of potentially great usefulness to Government policymakers is already being done by scholars independent of Government support altogether.

＊　　　　　　　＊　　　　　　　＊

THE NEED FOR "DANGEROUS TRUTHS"

Irving Louis Horowitz/Herbert Blumer

Congress has to concern itself with what may be an already dangerous imbalance between too much policy-oriented research and too little basic research. The legislative branch must take into account the fact that, even in advance of its creation, there is an impulse to view a national social-sciences foundation as a means to strengthen the hands of those who look upon the social sciences as simply national security resources. I think that Congress should see to it that the creation of still another agency does not give rise to the sort of unholy alliances that at times are established between virtually autonomous Federal agencies and the entrepreneurial empires scattered throughout the world of social science. It is a worthy objective that such an agency be neutral and not policy-oriented.

I don't think it is too early to search for answers to the problems that may immediately confront such an N.S.S.F. In the briefest possible way, we should like to examine at least a few of these. Doubtless, the committee will understand that these observations and queries are intended to be supportive of an N.S.S.F., since the encouragement of basic research in the social sciences is vital to the health of American society.

The nature of the social and behavioral sciences makes the sort of consensus about methodology and goals, which exists in the natural sciences, highly unlikely at this time.

Not in contention here is whether or not one chooses to describe the social sciences as continuous and contiguous with the natural sciences, or sharply breaking with the "non-human" sciences. It would not be the N.S.S.F.'s function to answer such conjectural matters, nor would its function be to hang too many research pegs on any one approach now fashionable. But such an organization should support studies to assist in settling these long-standing debates as to the proper nature and proper subject matter of the various sciences.

Turning to another matter, the conduct of basic social-science research deeply and directly affects policy issues and political sentiments. What is required is an appreciation that intellectual and ideological sensitivities are involved, and they cannot be ignored. To convert the meaning of pure social science into an operational codebook for noncontroversial social science would be self-defeating and even, in my opinion, suicidal.

There are already social-science organizations supporting nonsensitive research—such as the Twentieth Century Fund and the Bollingen Foundation. What should be encouraged by Congressional legislation is research into dangerous areas. The oversimplified identification of social science with natural-science techniques may lead away from this search for dangerous truths. Granting agencies should *not* assume that a noncontroversial and accommodating style is equivalent to a maximum yield in substantive findings.

We have a tradition, inherited from the feudal world, of *noblesse oblige* and of being very kind to one another because we live in a world in which words are, in our special breed of intellectual cats, equivalent to fists. We tend to be overly sensitive, needlessly solicitous, and as a result we tend not to be as intellectually sharp with one another as we ought to be.

The formation of an N.S.S.F. would involve a higher concentration of organizational energies, intellectual talent, and financial sources than has hitherto ever been the case in the social sciences. It is therefore extremely important that social-science research facilities be strictly maintained on a pluralistic basis. Care should be taken to prevent the multiple forms of social-science research from being smothered or obscured by the development of a monolithic agency committed to a single, limited orientation.

We should encourage Congress to stimulate both the various policy-making and non-policy-making agencies to use basic social-science research findings and to originate social-science projects within legislative and executive agencies. The creation of an N.S.S.F. should be an occasion for vitalizing research services of existing organizations, not for demoralizing them. From the poverty program to the Pan-American Union, efforts to generate independent social-science research must be redoubled.

It would be easier to stimulate basic social-science research through an independent institution, such as an N.S.S.F., than to simply allocate more funds for policy agencies. The fact is that existing Federal departments are concerned, most of the time, with fostering special ends of their own rather than with the autonomous goals of the social sciences. Furthermore, there would be a strong foreign resistance to any work commissioned through an N.S.S.F. that had a direct policy commitment. The findings generated by a policy-oriented N.S.S.F. would more nearly represent an official line than anything now done by social scientists working under Federal grants or contracts. To avoid this possibility, the independent character of any

N.S.S.F. must be guaranteed as far as possible by legislative safeguards.

Such an organization should not be allowed to become a centralized research center that encourages consensualist responses and conforming research designs. These bureaucratic tendencies are not calculated to improve the breed of the social sciences. In any pluralistic democratic society, a certain strain between science and policy is not only inevitable but valuable.

This strain may provide a sounding-board of hard truths against which policy-making must echo its sentiments. American society would be far weaker if its policy decisions were exclusively guided by, say, public-opinion polls than by the gamut of social-scientific data now in use. To convert the proposed N.S.S.F. into an adjunct of policy is to run a grave risk of undermining its independence. This potential loss of intellectual nerve can easily occur when other avenues of Government financing of social-science research projects become narrowed. The creation of a new agency of social research should, therefore, be used to inform existing agencies of the need for basic social-science findings in the conduct of their own work. Not to do so may create a one-sided imbalance favoring present policy-research agencies over and against basic research requirements.

A "NEED FOR INCREASING COHESION"

Leland J. Haworth

The National Science Foundation was established in 1950 to foster and encourage basic research and education in all the sciences. At that time, it was not clear to the Congress or to others how far the Foundation ought to go in the social sciences. From the legislative history, it is clear that Congress felt that the Foundation itself ought to determine how fast and how far it should go.

In 1953, the Foundation began a study of a possible program in the social sciences comparable in every way to the ones in the natural sciences. The Foundation's first social-science program was approved in 1954. At first, support of the social sciences was confined to those areas that "converged" with the natural sciences. In 1956, however, the social sciences were given separate identity—the social-science research program was created, consolidating research support from all divisions and eliminating the criterion of "convergence."

In 1960 the Social Science Division was established, placing the social sciences on the same administrative level as the other divisions that existed at that time: biological and medical sciences, and mathematical, physical, and engineering sciences.

The social-sciences division, of course, was initially very small. It has grown in the last six or seven years much more rapidly than the Foundation's program as a whole. Since 1960 it has doubled. The fractional part of the Foundation's research funds that it represents is now growing at a rate of 15 percent or 20 percent a year. For the current year, it has reached a bit more than $20 million.

For the social sciences in 1968, we have requested an increase of not quite 25 percent. But we can't clearly spell the rest of our support for the social sciences. These other funds represent composite and varied support. I have in mind such things as our providing matching funds to assist universities in constructing buildings for their graduate programs, and our investment in education, including fellowships, teacher training and retraining, curriculum development, and undergraduate-research participation. You can never predict how the benefits will be distributed among natural science, social science, engineering, and so forth.

Our support goes clear across the spectrum of the social sciences. Initially not all disciplines were covered, but I think it is fair to say that all are covered now and that the proposals in any branch of the social sciences are welcome.

One important point should be noted. For some disciplines, such as archaeology and the history and philosophy of science, the Foundation has been practically the sole source of Federal research funds; for other disciplines, such as political science, economics, linguistics, and demography, the Foundation is the major source of basic, non-mission-oriented work.

In describing the Foundation's social-science research program and our criteria for it, let me first discuss two broad legislative boundaries that circumscribe the program and that are inherent in the Foundation's mission. First, all our research programs in the social sciences at the present time must be "basic" in nature. Second, they must be "scientific." (The National Science Foundation Act of 1950 authorizes the Foundation to initiate and support "basic scientific research.") The Foundation interprets this language broadly, however, and encourages a variety of research approaches to a wide range of subjects, including research projects that are problem-oriented—so long as the research promises to yield valid scientific generalizations, rather than find solutions to problems peculiar to a particular time, place, or event.

Nevertheless, certain areas of social-science research

are, at the present time, denied Foundation support. Applied or professional clinical studies are not eligible. This excludes the larger part of social work, clinical psychology, legal studies, and a very large percentage of overseas research that is primarily applied in nature. Applied social-science research, however, is supported by the Department of State, the Arms Control and Disarmament Agency, and the Peace Corps.

Fortunately, the percentage of research in social sciences that meets the criterion of being scientific has been growing. Experience has shown that although techniques of investigation may vary among different branches of social science, the spirit of objective and analytical inquiry is common to all. There is every reason to hope that patterns and regularities observable in the social scene will become increasingly amenable to objective analysis and ultimately to statement in the form of scientific laws.

The specific criteria that we apply in our support of basic-research projects in the social sciences are those that offer the best combination of encouragement for the advancement of human knowledge—combined with suitable safeguards against undesirable duplication, exceeding the bounds of legislative authority, and violation of standards of scholarly excellence and sound judgment.

I should say that, in common with all the Foundation's programs, the initiative for deciding what an individual is going to do research on really comes from him. We don't go out and tap people on the shoulder and say, "We would like you to do this kind of project or that kind of project," but use our influence in a general way.

I would like to turn now to a fairly broad statement

of the sort of thing we visualize for the future. We have given a lot of thought to this in the last year or two, and we were stimulated to further thought by the considerations that you and your committee have been giving to the social sciences.

We need to give additional support to centers for advanced specialized research, particularly those engaged in attacking multi-disciplinary problems. Some of these centers lead a precarious financial existence, and finding resources inevitably wastes professional time. We believe there needs to be a rationalization of their organization, financial basis, regional dispersion, and specialization, for they will shape research in the future even more than they have to the present.

The social sciences now have only one center of a national character—the Center for Advanced Study in the Behavioral Sciences at Stanford. The Center affords senior scholars a place to pursue advanced research or to write up research results away from their normal academic environment. A national center for social-science research located in Washington is also a recurrent theme. Certainly Washington contains vital material—both archival and living—that is inadequately exploited.

It is important that we expand also our support of basic social-science research in the underdeveloped world. At the present time, a wide range of disciplines are involved in comparative studies of social, psychological, economic, and political topics in Asia, Africa, and Latin America. All share a concern in understanding the problems of developing countries. There is, as yet, little coordination of these efforts.

We would like to help develop regional basic-research centers where the prospective overseas researcher would receive appropriate intensive training to supplement his own disciplinary competence. For example, an anthropologist could learn about the political structure of the country; a political scientist could learn about the social structure. Both groups might require special language training, whereas a linguist might require knowledge about the most appropriate ways of approaching natives.

In a different context, we propose to increase support for a special class of projects—to develop sets of methods or models for demonstrating new powers of analysis. Recently, a small number of individuals, organized as the Mathematical Social Science Board, developed a class of mathematical models that have brought new insights and approaches to bear on social-science training and research programs. The pattern is flexible and can be adapted to various levels of difficulty and to the needs of several social-science disciplines.

Now, all of these things can be done within the N.S.F.'s present authority. If our authority were broadened, we could increase our effectiveness. We have in mind authorization to undertake what could be called, in general, "applied research."

One example would be programs to bring social-science knowledge to social practitioners, such as local officials, police officers, social workers, and clergymen. We would also like to see social-science research incorporated into Federal, state, and local welfare programs—not just at the planning stage, but in the execution as well. A third area of extension we have considered is a combination of social-science engineering and natural sciences to attack technological problems, such as water and air pollution, the pressure of population, and the inadequacies of mass transportation. However, the time has come when we must move beyond the facile identification of promising research opportunities.

In addition, the National Endowment for the Humanities and the Foundation have agreed to establish cooperative arrangements for the joint support of projects straddling the spheres of responsibility of the two agencies.

Finally, I come to a position on the bill that you introduced, Senator Harris. First, I would like to say that although I am going to register a serious doubt about it, I recognize fully that it is a matter of opinion and judgment. It is one on which reasonable men can disagree, and a difficult thing to prove in either direction.

There is no question that a separate foundation for the social sciences would give the social sciences more visibility. Just the fact that a foundation of that name existed, dedicated to the social sciences, would have that effect. It might prove to be a center of intellectual stimulus. It would certainly provide another source of general funding. Whatever might be the net result in *total* funding, it would be done from a different, but not necessarily better, standpoint from that of other agencies.

On the other hand, we feel that there are serious difficulties, or potential difficulties, of which I believe the strongest is that there is a great need for increasing cohesion in this whole spectrum that I have been talking about. I have never believed that the two cultures are as sharply divided as our good British friend, C.P. Snow, expressed it, but I believe that there has not been enough mutuality of interest, not enough common viewpoint. Incidentally, this gap exists *within* the natural sciences and *within* the social sciences, as well as between the natural sciences and the social sciences and the natural sciences and engineering, and all of these and the humanities. There has not been enough integration, enough recognition, enough across-the-board scholarship and interest among these disciplines.

My principal concern about a separate foundation for the social sciences would be the splintering effect that it might have.

My second objection relates to the effectiveness of the Government operations in themselves. I question whether a separate agency is good from this standpoint. It certainly would have some drawbacks. I am wondering whether the advantages would be enough to make up for these drawbacks.

Now, I hasten to add that I am not saying that the Government agencies now engaging in social-science research should *not* be engaged in such research. But I do question whether there should be one agency engaged in the development of the underlying knowledge and understanding that the mission-oriented agencies as well as other public and private agencies need to help advance society and overcome some of its difficulties.

For there is some danger that, if a separate foundation were established, many of the more basic research programs of mission-oriented agencies and the N.S.F. would be viewed as redundant, with consequent cutbacks or limitations in their funding.

*   *   *

THE ARGUMENTS FOR AND AGAINST

Launor F. Carter

In the paragraphs that follow, I wish to consider a number of arguments in favor of the proposed foundation, as well as to comment on several that are used as arguments against the foundation.

Social scientists' aspirations need raising.

As has been well documented, most of the support for research and advanced development has been given to the physical and biological sciences. Social-science scientists have generally not aspired to the level of support required to develop the basic knowledge that can lead to a frontal attack on the many social problems facing our nation. Generally, social scientists have worked as single individuals and as part of the university academic departments, doing research within the limited resources available for small studies. They have been traditionally content with limited resources for individual study, for travel to collect data, or for relatively minor experimentation.

This limited attack on the various basic problems in the social sciences is not sufficiently productive; large, well-financed, and carefully organized projects must take the place of small, individual efforts. Social scientists will make this transition to project research only if they believe that sufficient support is available to undertake such efforts.

Social scientists need spokesmen who will present their needs and aspirations to the Administration and to Congress.

Within the present organization of the Office of

Science and Technology, the National Science Foundation, the research establishment of the Defense Department, and the Department of Health, Education, and Welfare, there are no social scientists who hold responsible senior positions *and* have as their mission the presentation of the case for extensive social-science research. While there *are* social scientists holding senior positions on some of these agencies, they are not primarily devoted and dedicated to furthering the cause of social-science research; their orientation is to the overall mission of the agency. Since the social sciences are so comparatively less well developed and understood than the physical and biological sciences, it is important that their needs and potential receive relatively greater support than some of the other scientific and research areas.

Better people need to be attracted to the social sciences.

It is often asserted that the better people are attracted to those areas of scientific specialization where there is great national interest and where resources allow them to undertake the kinds of studies that will make important contributions to intellectual understanding.

Recent material published by the Educational Testing Service shows that the natural sciences and social sciences attract equally good students as far as verbal aptitude is concerned, but the social-science students are significantly low in quantitative ability. I believe this lack of numerical aptitude hinders the development of a true research-based social science.

The level of funding for the social sciences needs to be radically increased.

Generally, the level of support for the social sciences

is between 5 percent and 10 percent of the level of support in other scientific areas. The total level of Federal support for social sciences is around $325 million, with over half representing funds coming from the U.S. Office of Education for research in education. In 1966, the N.S.F. supported social-science activities to the extent of $29.7 million out of a budget of $466 million, or 6.4 percent.

In this respect, it is important to note that the N.S.F. lumps together all of the social sciences: Economics, political science, sociology, anthropology, social psychology, and so on, go into one category to arrive at the $29 million. But in the physical sciences each one is treated separately: Mathematics receives $45 million, physics $50 million, chemistry $40 million, astronomy $24 million, and so on. In other words, the level of support of social science, considered collectively, was less than that of a number of other single disciplines in the physical sciences. It appears that we put our major support in those areas where our understanding is highest, rather than in those where it is lowest and needs the greatest improvement.

The cost of experimental social-science studies is high and increasing.

It is often argued that social-science research is relatively inexpensive. Once this was the case, but modern empirical social-science research, if properly done, *is* expensive. Empirical social science depends on the collection and extensive analysis of data. At times it involves experimental manipulation, which—if done in real-life situations—is quite expensive. The cost of collecting survey information on any large representative population runs into thousands of dollars. Maintaining of large data banks by modern information-processing techniques costs hundreds of thousands of dollars a year.

Historical and theoretical social science needs support.

At the present time, there are only modest sums available to support social-science research that is oriented toward empirical investigations. But there are only *minute* funds available for the support of those social scientists whose orientation is essentially historical and theoretical. Their ability to obtain such simple things as adequate library support, clerical support, or even time away from their teaching duties is often very limited.

As the committee is well aware, there are a significant number of social and natural scientists who oppose the formation of a separate social-science foundation. I would like to consider two of the arguments they commonly advance.

Good ideas in the social sciences receive adequate support now.

It is often argued that, under the current levels of funding, any social scientist of repute who has good ideas receives adequate support. There is some truth to this, and it represents a contradictory dilemma regarding the social sciences.

It is true that many social scientists are being supported by the N.S.F., the N.I.H., and the Defense Department. This funding is at a level that is reasonable, in terms of these scientists' current needs and current conception of the support needed to perform social-science studies.

I would argue, however, that this is a result of the fact that for many years social scientists received next to no support, and thus were unable to plan or think in terms of experimental work truly adequate to the phenomena they were studying. There are many important theories in the social sciences having to do with delinquency, crime, housing, urban affairs, social organization, disarmament, and so forth, that have never been attacked with the vigor and intensity they should be attacked with—because funds were simply not available to allow researchers to undertake a long-range, intensive study of these areas.

Science should not be divided.

There are those who contend that it is unwise to set up a separate foundation for the social sciences—on the grounds that the N.S.F. has established a Social Science Division, and is giving increasing support to this division. Further, with adequate support from the Administration and Congress, the N.S.F. will increase its attention to this area.

My experience with the N.S.F. indicates that all of this is true, and that the director and deputy director have the best of intentions regarding the support of the social sciences. Nevertheless, the N.S.F., with its historic orientation in the physical and biological sciences, cannot furnish the dedicated and focused leadership the social sciences need. The social sciences need their own protagonists in the highest levels of Government, simply because the development of a powerful understanding of our social problems is a matter of the first importance.

In addition, it is sometimes asserted that the social sciences, the biological sciences, and the physical sciences should all be under the same roof, since they represent the totality of the scientific discipline. To the extent that this argument is based on mere propinquity, it does not stand careful scrutiny. The contribution of the physical and biological sciences to most social science is relatively small, since most of the social sciences are relatively unrelated to the new developments or new advances in the physical and biological sciences.

In summary, Mr. Chairman, it is my belief that the arguments in favor of the establishment of a national social-science foundation greatly overweigh the arguments opposing such a foundation.

January/February 1968

The Need for a
National Social Science
Foundation

FRED R. HARRIS

In again introducing the National Social Science Foundation Act, this time with the cosponsorship of 32 senators, I would like to explain briefly why we believe that now is the time to redefine the way in which social science research, education, training and scholarship should be supported by the federal government.

The bill declares as national policy that the encouragement and support of research, education, training and scholarship in the social sciences is a matter of great concern to the federal government; it underscores the importance of the social sciences in dealing with the concerns of the nation; and it creates a new instrument to effect a rapidly expanded, yet balanced, program of support.

The foundation would be comprised of a board of trustees consisting of 24 prominent citizens from the social

This essay is an edited version of remarks made on the floor of the Senate, January 22, 1969.

science community, both academic and practicing. There would be, as well, a director and a deputy director, appointed by the President with the advice and consent of the Senate.

The foundation would do no in-house research but would, in keeping with the precedent set by the National Science Foundation and the National Foundation for the Arts and Humanities, underwrite, fund and support academic research, education and training in political science, economics, psychology, sociology, anthropology, history, law, social statistics, demography, geography, linguistics, communication, international relations, education and other social sciences. The scope of the program of the foundation will, therefore, allow for support of the social sciences under the broadest possible definition. Funds would support the development of institutions as well as research projects selected on the basis of individual merit.

Largely because of the repercussions after public disclosure of Project Camelot and similar projects funded by the defense and intelligence agencies, inquiry into the support of such research by federal agencies was held, starting shortly after March 1, 1966, by the Senate Subcommittee on Government Research, of which I am chairman.

The conclusions reached by the end of the hearings were that it was necessary to create an alternate source of support not only in order to "civilianize" foreign-area research but to foster the overall development of social science capability. We found that, because of inadequate funds, scholars who desire to conduct foreign-area research often seek support from defense and intelligence agencies, or, in many cases, do not accomplish their research. Furthermore, neither the National Science Foundation nor the other relevant federal agencies have been able to sustain the level of funding necessary to underwrite the training and the research of increasing numbers of graduate students and postdoctoral researchers.

The subcommittee identified several key issues during hearings held over the last two sessions of Congress that would begin to be resolved by the creation of an independent governmental agency designed to nurture and support social science research, education and training.

1. The social sciences need more federal support for research and development. In 1966 the social sciences received only 2.4 percent of all basic research funded by the federal government. The estimated obligations for 1967 and 1968 were about the same —2.5 percent for both years. The portion of federal support for applied social science research out of the total is not much different—3.5 percent in 1966, 3.6 percent in 1967, 3.7 percent in 1968.

2. The National Science Foundation has given very little or no support at all to certain methodologies and disciplines within the social sciences. It did not even start a political science program until 11 years after the beginning of formal support of social sciences. NSF has maintained a decidedly hard—that is *natural* science—bias toward its social science program. While this is understandable for an agency with a natural science orientation, it does not follow that what is good for the natural and physical sciences is necessarily the best for the social sciences. An adverse consequence is the frequent sacrifice of relevance for rigor, and the accumulation of "hard" social data that may well not increase knowledge of the critical social problems of our nation.

3. The social sciences have suffered from insufficient attention to their development, visibility and prestige, not only because of the reasons given above, but be-

cause of the failure to recognize fully the potential importance and significant contribution they can make to the achievement of national goals. A new foundation with specific authority would encourage a quantum leap in funding for the social sciences and revitalize social science research conducted by other federal agencies.

4. Innovative and perhaps controversial thinking and research must be encouraged in the social sciences if the nation hopes to meet the challenges of the pressing and growing social problems that face it. The National Science Foundation, with about 90 percent of its basic research budget directed toward the natural sciences, will continue to find it difficult to promote such research in the social sciences. A strong legislative mandate to encourage innovative research will give the social sciences the confidence they need and deserve, and the authority they must have.

5. Interdisciplinary and multidisciplinary research must be conducted on a much greater scale in universities and other research organizations. Many modern problems do not fall neatly within the boundaries of a single discipline. One of the barriers to collaboration and cooperation between the natural and social sciences has, in the past, been the inferior status of the latter. A new foundation will serve to foster interdisciplinary research and, in the long run, unify the sciences.

At the same time we do not conceive that the proposed foundation should become the exclusive federal supporter of social science research. All agencies of the federal government now supporting social science research—including the National Science

Foundation and the National Foundation for the Arts and Humanities—will continue to support and, indeed, increase their level of support for the social sciences.

6. The nation cannot adequately confront its myriad social problems without more social science knowledge. Social conditions are constantly being altered by rapidly developing science and technology, population growth and the hastening deterioration of urban America made more critical every day by continued movement of youth from rural America to the already overburdened cities. For example, we need to learn how and why discontent and alienation are generated in a society with such a high degree of general affluence, and why unemployment and poverty persist despite increasing efforts to solve them. Answers to these questions will not come easily, but they will come much more quickly if support for social science research is sharply increased, and if the social sciences are encouraged to probe to the root.

Some argue that statistics show a proper balance of federal support for the social and natural sciences, based on the relative capabilities of each. The subcommittee agrees, however, with Dr. Rensis Likert, Director of the Institute of Social Research, University of Michigan, who took the opposite position in our hearings. He said that

. . . The rapidly increasing number of younger, well-trained social scientists . . . are prepared to accomplish much or little, depending on the resources we provide for their use.

Dr. Gerald Holton, Department of Physics, Harvard University, underscored this point:

. . . in the next 30 years there will be 10 to 20 times the number of people wanting to do basic research in the social sciences, and . . . they will make a very good case for the meaningful expenditures of 20 to 50 times the amount of 1967 dollars.

Private foundations have severely limited funds and cannot keep up with the influx of students and research proposals. The Social Science Research Council, for example, can finance only a small percentage of the good research applications they receive. Dr. Austin Ranney, Chairman of the Committee on Governmental and Legal Processes, Social Science Research Council, testified that, under a five-year grant from the Ford Foundation, the Council has approximately $60,000 a year to allocate to all research applications under the jurisdiction of his committee and that for the year 1967 they had 53 applications, totaling $590,595, which were considered meritorious and worthy of support.

Even within the social sciences there are "have" and "have not" disciplines and methodologies. Dr. James A. Robinson, Director, Mershon Center for Education in National Security, Ohio State University, identified three approaches to political science research: nonscience, science and policy:

. . . research on norms, science, and policy ought to share in public support for their work on the basis of competence, not on the basis of what is available. Hence, it is regrettable that those concerned with norms are served by one foundation (Humanities), those concerned with science another (NSF), and those concerned with policy none at all.

Creation of the NSSF would emphasize that the federal government is committed to support all social science disciplines and recognized methodologies on a continuing basis and to provide the social sciences with the recognition they need and deserve. Some argue that gradual equalization can be achieved by beefing up the social sciences within the NSF and mission-oriented agencies. I do not consider this realistic; nor would it alter, in most cases, the present reliance of social science on the judgment, understanding and support of natural scientists. I find no reason to believe that physical scientists are necessarily endowed with the special insights needed to develop the social sciences.

Others have advanced the argument that a separate social science foundation would encourage other agencies of the government to decrease support for social science research. The subcommittee disagrees, and experience supports our view. The recently created National Foundation for the Arts and Humanities shares overlapping responsibility with the National Science Foundation in several areas of scholarship including history and linguistics; yet the National Science Foundation has actually increased its support for research in these areas. And Dr. Leland J. Haworth, director of the Foundation, testified that it is his intention to continue to increase and expand the Foundation's support for such research. Similar testimony was heard from almost every official who testified on behalf of the mission-oriented agencies of the federal government.

Such a "credit-debit" view of government operations, which maintains that an increase in social science research funds from one agency means a reduction from another, is simplistic and unsupported by fact or history.

With the passage of this bill, the social sciences will receive a place in the higher councils of government. As Dr. Launor Carter, vice president, Systems Development Corporation, testified:

. . . senior members of the social sciences profession

[will] be in key positions in government so that the role and potential contribution of social science can be forcefully presented in administrative councils.

The NSSF bill is also designed to encourage the social sciences to develop to their full potential. Dr. Vincent Davis, Graduate School of International Studies, University of Denver, testified:

. . . Diversified sources of support provide a number of places where dissenting minority groups can seek help. Diversified sources, therefore, represent within the scientific and scholarly world a crudely approximate equivalent to the checks and balances provided within our political system by having more than one political party. . . .

The degree of difficulty should not cause us to turn away from attempting better basic understanding of the problems. We have learned from our massive space effort, for example, that the success of an operational program is significantly dependent upon the scope and comprehensiveness of the underlying research activities. As Dr. Ross Stagner, chairman of the department of psychology, Wayne State University, has said:

We have been spending (justifiably) millions of dollars on urban renewal. But we have made little use of the expertise of economists, sociologists, and psychologists with respect to planning for human welfare, not just for buildings. . . . I do feel very strongly that the knowledge of social scientists ought to be given much higher consideration than it has. . . . [We] simply have not investigated the problems of urban renewal from the viewpoint of neighborhood unity, of social supports for behavior codes, of communication networks, of leader-follower relations, and a mass of other important factors. There is still so much ignorance, and so much misinformation disguised as "common-sense," that one can hardly be surprised at the unsatisfactory consequences of these programs.

As strong as the case has been for swift passage of this legislation, events in the Congress and elsewhere subsequent to the hearings of the subcommittee have made favorable arguments even more compelling.

A report of the Panel of Defense, Social and Behavioral Sciences released in 1967 calling for, among other things, more emphasis on "peacefare" research prompted the Chairman of the Senate Foreign Relations Committee, the Senator from Arkansas, to engage in an exchange of letters with Dr. John S. Foster, Director, Defense Research and Engineering. In Foster's reply to the letter and in subsequent hearings on the matter he clearly asserted that:

Some of the work (in the social sciences) which we support would not be required if the information were available or were being developed outside the Department of Defense. . . .

In consonance with the above statement, Foster also indicated: "If other agencies expanded their programs in areas relevant to our needs, we would reconsider our effort."

But a shift of the funding pattern of social science research does not come about automatically with any degree of permanence without a Congressional mandate.

That a spokesman for the social sciences in the form of a new agency is needed now more than ever before was also demonstrated during the Senate appropriation hearings on the National Science Foundation for fiscal year 1969. Their authority to support the social sciences was questioned, particularly in the area of the controversial discipline, political science. When a very small percentage of an agency's total research budget can threaten the major share of its funds, then the agency's course of action is only natural—take no chances, support noncontroversial, non-innovative, lackluster and possibly irrelevant research in the social sciences.

Some argue that the act reorganizing the National Science Foundation, which was passed into law last session, significantly enhances the position of the social sciences. I disagree, not with the motives of the very able people involved but, again, with the premise that the National Science Foundation is the best home for the social sciences.

The present mandate to support the social sciences is not only vague, but the legislative history specifically directs the NSF not to give "a disproportionate amount" of support. The increasing demands on the social sciences cannot be met by an agency thus limited. Even under the most favorable developments imaginable within the National Science Foundation, it will be many years before the established institutional arrangements between the scientific community and the federal government ensure anything but that the natural and physical sciences will continue to command all but a small share of federal research money.

In conclusion, let me ask the question: Who spoke for the social sciences when the research and development budget was severely cut last year? The answer is: No one. Who in the federal government will be looking out for the best interests of the social sciences during another year of apparently keen competition for funds? No one —not unless a separate agency is created.

The extensive Congressional interest in the social sciences since the Camelot affair of 1965 has given them more visibility. But they continue to be treated as poor relatives, and the absence of a Congressional mandate has made it impossible for them to improve their position. Will the social sciences retain their second-class citizenship or will

Congress rise to the occasion and realize that it must enact legislation to guarantee a healthy and viable growth of the social sciences on a continuing basis? Such a goal is achievable with the passage of the National Foundation for the Social Sciences Act of 1969.

May 1969

NOTES ON CONTRIBUTORS

Herbert Blumer ("The Need for Dangerous Truths") is professor of sociology at the University of California at Berkeley. His most recent book is *Essays in Symbolic Interaction.*

Launor F. Carter ("The Arguments For and Against") is senior vice-president of System Development Corporation. He is chief scientist for the United States Air Force, and is the author of numerous articles which have appeared in professional journals. He has been a consulting editor of *Psychology Bulletin* and the *Journal of Abnormal and Social Psychology,* and associate editor of *Sociometry.*

Kenneth B. Clark ("'. . . the Interests of the Privileged Are at Stake'") is a psychologist and the director of the Social Dynamics Reserach Institute, City College of New York. He is the author of *Dark Ghetto* and editor of *Encounter.*

Robert Coles ("Life in Appalachia—The Case of Hugh Mc-Caslin") is a research psychiatrist at Harvard University. He has published widely in the field of child psychiatry and is the author of three volumes of *Children in Crisis* entitled: *A Study of Courage and Fear; Migrants, Sharecroppers, Mountaineers;* and *The South Goes North.*

Herbert J. Gans (" 'There Is Still Time . . . But Not Much Time . . . ' ") is senior research sociologist at the Center for Urban Education in New York City. His most recent book is *People and Plans: Essays on Urban Problems and Solutions.*

Fred Harvey Harrington ("A 'Major Step' in America's Progress") is president of the University of Wisconsin. He is author of: *God, Mammon and the Japanese: Dr. Horace N. Allen and Korean-American Relations (1884-1905); Fighting Politician: Major General N. P. Banks;* and is co-author of *An American History, Hanging Judge* and *History of American Civilization.*

Fred R. Harris ("Building a New Social Strategy" and "The Need for a National Social Science Foundation") has represented Oklahoma in the United States Senate since 1964. For further information, see the cover.

Leland J. Haworth ("A 'Need for Increasing Cohesion' ") was director of the National Science Foundation, and is now special assistant to the president at Associated Universities, Inc., Upton, New York. He is the author of numerous articles for professional scientific journals.

Irving Louis Horowitz ("The Need for Dangerous Truths") is professor of sociology at Rutgers University. He is editor-in-chief of *Society* (formerly *trans*action) magazine and director of *Studies in Comparative International Development.* Among his recent books are *Foundations of Political Sociology, Three Worlds of Development* (2nd ed.) and *Cuban Communism,* published by Transaction Books.

Charlayne A. Hunter ("On the case in Resurrection City") was one of two black students who integrated the University of Georgia in 1961. She has worked for the *New Yorker,* was a Russell Sage Fellow at *trans*action (now SOCIETY), has worked at NBC television news in Washington, D.C., and is presently a reporter for the *New York Times.*

Bruce Jackson ("In the Valley of the Shadows: Kentucky") professor of English at State University of New York at Buffalo, is author of *Outside the Law: A Thief's Primer* published by Transaction Books and *Wake Up Dead Man,* a collection and analysis of Texas convict worksongs.

Milton Kotler ("Making Local Government Truly Local") is a political scientist associated with the Institute for Policy Studies, Washington, D.C. He is author of *Neighborhood Government: The Local Foundations of Political Life.*

Michael Lipsky ("Riot Commission Politics") is assistant professor of political science at the University of Wisconsin and a staff associate of the Institute for Research on Poverty. He wrote *Protest in City Politics.*

Theodore R. Marmor ("FAP Flop: The Fate of Nixon's Welfare Reform Proposals") teaches public policy courses at the University of Minnesota. Author of *The Politics of Medicare* and editor of *Poverty Policy,* he is interested in welfare state politics.

S. M. Miller ("Poverty Programs and Policy Priorities") is professor of education and sociology at New York University. He has been a government consultant on poverty, social change and school dropouts. He is co-author of *The Future of Inequality, Applied Sociology* and *Social Class and Social Policy.*

Walter F. Mondale ("Reporting on the Social State of the Union") has been U.S. Senator from Minnesota since 1964. He serves on Senate committees on space, agriculture, banking and currency, and aging. He led the fight for passage of the fair housing bill and fair warning law requiring manufacturers to notify automobile owners of safety defects.

Daniel P. Moynihan ("The Urban Negro *Is* the 'Urban Problem'") has worked in the Johnson and the Nixon Administrations. He is professor of education and urban politics at the Harvard University Graduate School of Education. Author of many journal articles, he has written *Maximum Feasible Understanding* and is co-author of *Beyond the Melting Pot.*

Dorothy Nelkin ("Invisible Migrant Workers"), senior research associate in the Cornell University program on Science, Technology and Society, worked on a migrant labor project with William H. Friedland and co-authored with him *Migrant: Agricultural Workers in America's Northeast.* She is doing research on technological decisions connected with nuclear power, housing innovation and methadone treatment.

David J. Olson ("Riot Commission Politics") is assistant professor of political science and director of undergraduate studies at Indiana University. He has conducted a number of studies on the impact of racial violence and is co-editor of and a contributor to *Black Politics: The Inevitability of Conflict.*

John M. Plank ("Who Uses U.S. Sponsored Research?") is director of Political Development Studies at the Brookings Institution. His main research interests are Latin American politics, government and political development, nationalism in societies which are changing rapidly, recruitment of political leaders in developing societies, and United States and Latin American relations.

Lee Rainwater ("The Services Strategy vs. the Income Strategy") is professor of sociology in the Department of Sociology and John F. Kennedy School of Government at Harvard University. A prolific author, his works include: *Workingman's Wife: Her Personality, World and Life Styles; Behind Ghetto Walls;* and *Soul,* published by Transaction Books.

Martin Rein ("Poverty Programs and Policy Priorities," "FAP Flop: The Fate of Nixon's Welfare Reform Proposals") is a professor in the Department of Urban Studies and Planning at MIT. Author of many works on public policy, poverty, the welfare state and housing, his most recent book is entitled *Social Policy: Issues of Choice and Change.*

Dankwart A. Rustow ("Improving Federally Funded Research") is professor of International Social Forces at Columbia University.

He is co-author of *Political Modernization in Japan and Turkey* and is author of *Politics of Compromise* and *A World of Nations*.

W. Willard Wirtz ("Public Uninterest in Social Science") was Secretary of Labor from 1962 to 1969. He is author of *Labor and the Public Interest*.